What others are say
God's Best During Yo

"Robin's story is brutally honest and transparent about the reality of pain and brokenness. But as you take this journey with her one thing is unmistakable, the love, mercy and companionship of Christ."
~ Sheila Walsh, inspirational speaker and author,
In the Middle of the Mess

"Robin's story is full of honesty and transparency. It showcases both the power and beauty of God's grace as well as staying true to the rawness of what it's like to experience brokenness and pain."
~ Jarrid Wilson, pastor, author, and
inspirational speaker

"God's Best During You Worst, is a scenario none of us ask for. Yet it's a place many of us have found ourselves. Author Robin Luftig has willingly gone back to that time in her life and gleaned life-sustaining hope to share with the rest of us. Her insight into difficult times is founded on biblical truth and delivered with humility and love. This is a book to cherish over and over again."
~ Edie Melson, award-winning author and
Director of the Blue Ridge Mountains
Christian Writers Conference

"Robin Luftig's book, *God's Best During Your Worst,* reminds us all that we have two choices with God: we can either doubt Him or we can trust Him. We can either try to hold all the cards ourselves, which means trying to *fix* it, or we can surrender and allow God to show us just how much He loves us (more than we can imagine). This is a book for everyone!"
~ Eva Marie Everson, bestselling author & speaker
and President of Word Weavers International

"Robin Luftig's *God's Best During Your Worst* packs a beautiful spiritual punch. Boom. Didn't see that coming. Taking us on a journey through her own worst of the worst, Robin guides us to the glorious truth of a God who is there. So very there. Best of times or worst of times, there's much to ponder here to help each of us with our own bests and worsts."

~ Rhonda Rhea, award-winning humor columnist, TV personality, author of 18 books

"Blindsided. Have you ever been blindsided by terrible news, a crippling rejection, a sudden loss, or a devastating diagnosis? Then you know what Robin Luftig knows—that it's not always easy to answer God when He asks, "Do you trust me?" Gripping writing, transparent honesty, raw revelation, and powerful truth. That's what you'll find inside the pages of *God's Best During Your Worst* as Robin tells the story of how she learned her answer. None of us know what tomorrow will bring. Prepare now by pressing into God today."

~ Lori Stanley Roeleveld, blogger, speaker, author of *The Art of Hard Conversations: Biblical Tools for the Tough Talks that Matter*

"When faced with tragedy we have two choices: become consumed or become a conqueror. In *God's Best During Your Worst,* Robin Luftig shares with vulnerability and openness the mental, emotional, and spiritual questions we ask of ourselves and of God when we're faced with situations that are too big for us to deal with on our own. No matter your struggle, *God's Best* will give you the hope you need by offering hope, reflection, and the reminder that with God on our side, we are already victorious.

~ Bethany Jett, award-winning co-author of *Platinum Faith: Live Brilliant, Be Resilient and Know Your Worth*

GOD'S BEST

during
your worst

GOD'S
BEST
during
your worst

LIVING UNDER HIS UMBRELLA

Robin Luftig

Bold Vision Books
PO Box 2011
Friendswood, Texas 77549

Book Dedication

My life's symphony began in June 1955,
but reached a fevered pitch in April 2011.
May God continue to conduct
His love through the rest of my days.

This book is dedicated to my dad,
Junior G. Gilbert.
He showed God to me in ways
nobody else ever did.

Table of Contents

Foreword~11

The Big Question~13

Chapter One – Moment of Truth~15

Chapter Two – Confusion~25

Chapter Three – Doubt~35

Chapter Four – Focus~45

Chapter Five – Trust~55

Chapter Six – Heartache~67

Chapter Seven – Surrender~77

Chapter Eight – Faith~

Chapter Nine – Gratitude~97

Chapter Ten – Peace~107

Chapter Eleven – Grace~115

Chapter Twelve – Now What~125?

Chapter Thirteen – Lived Promises: God at His Best~135

God is Trustworthy~153

Practicing Gratitude~161

About the Author~167

Endnotes~169

Foreword

Dr. Michelle Bengtson
Board Certified Clinical Neuropsychologist

*H*ave you ever experienced a trial so great it turned life upside down and inside out or left you wondering how long you had to live? How would you spend your time? To whom would you turn?

As a neuropsychologist, I see thousands of patients who struggle with diagnoses ranging from attention deficit hyperactivity disorder, autism, and learning disabilities to brain tumors, traumatic brain injury, and dementia. When they receive a diagnosis, there is often a mixture of emotion, from relief to fear. Relief often comes from just knowing what has been causing their symptoms and knowing that treatment exists. And yet the relief is often quickly replaced by the unknown of all that is yet to be faced. I often wonder how anyone faces such difficulties without a saving knowledge of Jesus Christ and faith in God, who promises to be with us at all times.

Having seen many patients face such circumstances, I can tell you we never quite know how we'll respond until we're faced with the situation.

In *God's Best During Your Worst: Living Under His Umbrella*, Robin uses the story of her brain tumor diagnosis and the ten days that followed as a platform to offer insight about how to handle tragedy. She shares the real-life questions, fears, and other emotions she battled as she faced the possibility that either the tumor or the treatment would claim her life. And during that time, she had to come to grips with her honest beliefs about herself and her God. She also includes stories of others who faced unfathomable tragedies yet found their way through with the help of knowing a living God.

While I know of no one who would desire to go through such an ordeal, I suspect that if you asked Robin now, she would tell you that, in many respects, what she gained through the experience was worth anything she lost in the process. For the process drew her closer to her husband, her children, and her God—the God who desires to use our trials to increase our faith and perfect our faith so that we will ultimately be complete in Him. Because that's what allows us to count these experiences, like Robin's, all joy.

James 1:2-4 reminds us, "Consider it pure joy, my brothers and sisters, whenever you face trials of many kinds, because you know that the testing of your faith produces perseverance. Let perseverance finish its work so that you may be mature and complete, not lacking anything."

What a challenge it is to see joy in the midst of trouble. But our chances of doing so are increased if we will rely on the One who will not only carry us through the difficulties but will also perfect our faith in the process.

May you also consider it pure joy, no matter where you are and what you face, so that ultimately you will be lacking in nothing.

Dr. Michelle Bengtson,
Board Certified Clinical Neuropsychologist
Author, *Hope Prevails: Insights from a Doctor's*
Personal Journey Through Depression

The Big Question

*I*n the spring of 2011 during a five-hour distraction-free drive to speak at a women's conference, God whispered in my heart a fundamental question about our relationship.

Do you trust Me?

Four words that changed my life forever.

For the rest of the drive, I pondered God's provision and whether He is a God worth loving. I knew the opportunity to share with these women was a direct result of God's goodness. Yet when I pulled into the conference center's driveway, I had to answer His question—*Do you trust Me?*—with a big "I don't know."

Maybe you picked up this book because you also question God's grace and mercy ... especially during tragic times.

Maybe you feel like your heart was ripped to shreds and you have no idea which way to go and what to believe.

Maybe your life was perfect ... until it suddenly wasn't.

I wrote this book specifically for you, to tell you there are opportunities waiting that can bring healing to your situation— *you* can heal.

When God whispered, *Do you trust Me?* during that long car ride, I wish I could say I answered Him with a resounding, "Yes, I trust You, no matter what."

But I didn't.

Little did I know I would soon face the worst experience of my life.

Chapter One

Moment of Truth

Journal entry: Saturday, April 2, 2011, 2:30 a.m.

I arrived at the hospital last night by ambulance. The waiting areas were crazy-busy with people everywhere. Gurneys and wheelchairs lined the hallways—each holding patients with a variety of ailments.

Wish they could change emergency room smells. They are always the same: a mixture of antiseptics, urine, and vomit.

See you upstairs honey," I called over my shoulder as I headed to bed. "And don't forget to set up the bikes."

Deciding to marry again after so many years of being single was one of the best decisions I'd ever made. Lew brought balance to my life. His motto: work hard, but remember to play.

Our Friday dinner-out ritual gave us the opportunity to talk and laugh. We usually chose a secluded restaurant booth. There, we'd shake off the tensions of the week, his as a business analyst and mine an executive assistant to a college vice president. Our goal was to pull our focus forward.

The weather report offered the promise of perfect weather—no rain in sight—for a bike ride the next morning, so a good night's sleep was a priority. Under the covers, I snuggled into the pillows, smooshing the fluff of the down into a just-right position. Lew lagged behind to check on our pets, set out our bikes, and lock the doors.

God had blessed me with a wonderful life. A perfect life.

As I waited for my husband and held the edge of my pillow, I realized my right hand clung tight. It wouldn't let go—*couldn't* let go.

This is odd.

Stretched out on my side, I squinted in the dim light at my hand. I saw my fingers curled, clenching the feathery pillow in a death grip.

What a whopper of a cramp.

I skootched onto my left elbow. With my free hand, I tried to pry my right fingers open. They would not release. Even as I tugged, there was no pain from my clenched hold, but loosening its grasp proved to be impossible.

After several moments, I gave a yank and jerked the pillow out of my grip. That's when my hand began moving on its own, slowly twisting outward. Moments later, my arm began to bend, first at the wrist then contorting, rotating away from my body.

A pitiful wisp of air escaped my lips in a pathetic attempt to scream. Excruciating pain seared through me. Still my arm twisted, spastic and palsied. Terrified, I thought I would soon hear bones snap. Nothing relieved my pain or the contortions.

What's wrong with me? Am I having a stroke? Am I going to die? Is God bringing me home?

Sounds of Lew's steps tapped on the hallway floor outside our room. The instant he walked in, I made eye contact and silently pleaded for help. Shock registered on his face. He rushed to my side and tried to open my grip and straighten my arm.

"Call 9-1-1," I gasped a rough, airy noise.

The words had barely escaped my lips when my entire body began flailing, resembling a toy controlled by some insane puppeteer.

After Lew made a quick call to 9-1-1, he knelt at my side, watching and waiting for the seizure to pass. After what felt like an eternity, the twitching and thrashing waned. My arm relaxed. My breathing became less labored. Lew carefully pulled me close. We held each other, willing our fear away.

Reflections of flashing ambulance lights glowed through the window and pulsated against the bedroom wall.

I'll be fine now. Help is here.

Dead Weight

When the EMTs entered the bedroom, they immediately checked my vitals.

"Your pulse and heart rate are racing a bit, Mrs. Luftig, but that's to be expected," one of them said offhandedly. "Your body is reacting to trauma." Neither of the medical team appeared alarmed, so I began to relax.

Slowly, I regained my voice. The EMTs and I maintained a strained level of small talk while they continued their examination. They wrapped a blood pressure cuff on my right arm, noted a higher than normal elevation in my blood pressure, and attributed it to my body's response to the trauma.

Once the EMT removed the cuff, however, my arm dropped onto the bed. Instantly their demeanor changed. Chatter stopped. They began working in double-time. One of them snatched the sheets off me and reached for my legs.

"Can you wiggle your toes?" he asked. My left foot responded, but my right foot remained motionless.

"Move your right leg, Mrs. Luftig."

Again, no response.

A deep dread washed over me. "I don't understand." Strangers stood in my bedroom, but I had little time or inclination to concern myself with clothes draped over the chair or other housekeeping faux pas. This was all business.

"Grasp my hands; use *both* of them. Reach for me."

My left fingers reached effortlessly toward him, but my right arm and hand remained motionless.

Dead weight.

I willed my arm to move. I tried to wiggle my fingers—the fingers that had just moments ago resembled curled talons—even tried to move my legs and wriggle my toes, but the right side of my body refused to cooperate.

Realization hit hard—my right side was paralyzed.

The EMTs wasted no time. They expertly moved me onto the gurney and rushed me to the ambulance.

As I entered the hospital, an ER nurse assigned me to a private curtained room, where Lew and I attempted to comfort each other. To make sense of the paralysis and seizure.

"Good evening, Mrs. Luftig," Dr. Rupen Modi said as he threw back the curtain, entering my room. "What brings you here today?"

His kind demeanor calmed me, and I immediately felt at peace. *This man will find out what's wrong. I'll be just fine.*

After Dr. Modi's initial evaluation of my symptoms and multiple questions, he shared his conclusion.

"Seems you've suffered a mini stroke. People have them more times than you think," he said. "It may be something you'll learn to deal with."

It was as if all the air left the room. The thought of never knowing when I could experience the same loss of control stole my breath.

"I don't know what I just experienced," I said through tears, "but there's no way I can learn to live with *that*. There has to be a reason for what happened!"

Moment of Truth

Dr. Modi ordered an MRI,[1] and I willed myself to relax. We waited for the results.

---

1   Magnetic Resonance Imaging

By 4 a.m. I had regained control on my right side, with only a veiled numbness lingering on my right-hand fingertips.

Even with the intruding lights and hectic noises from the nurses' station outside our curtained hideout, Lew and I dozed as we awaited the end to this nightmare.

We roused when Dr. Modi returned to my room, ashen-faced, eyes focused on the floor, not looking to either Lew or me. He walked to the right side of my bed and placed two pieces of paper face down beside me. He then lifted his gaze to meet mine.

"I'm so sorry, Mrs. Luftig," he said in a soft voice as he reached for my hand, stroking the top of it ever so gently, "You have a tumor on your brain."

What?

"The tests show you experienced a massive seizure. Right now, we're quite sure the tumor caused it—"

Tumor?

"You did not suffer a mini stroke as we first thought—"

I have a tumor?

"It's much more serious. The tumor on your brain is about the size of a man's fist—"

A brain tumor?

"We'll schedule you with a neurosurgeon later today—"

I can't have a brain tumor.

"My colleagues and I are relatively confident the surgeon will order more tests, but my guess is you'll need surgery within a week or two. This is not my area of expertise—I'm an emergency medicine doctor." He raked his hair with his fingers. "And I don't know neurology's surgical schedule." He picked up the pictures and stared at them. "But I know this much. You must remove that tumor before it causes any more damage. Don't hold me to it, but you're probably looking at surgery in ten days."

Ten days? You can't be serious. Is this a joke?

Lew and I stared at each other, then turned back to the doctor.

"What are you saying? I can't have a tumor on my brain. There must be some mistake. I've been fine." I willed my declaration to make it so.

With that, Dr. Modi picked the two papers from the bed and handed them to me. They were two black-and-white MRI scanned images. From the side and back views, the bones of my skull glowed white against the black film. I easily located the dark areas of my eye socket and sinus cavity. Behind them sat the folds and wrinkles of my brain.

Then I spotted it.

My tumor.

Amidst the brain matter, a light gray mass more than twice the size of my eye socket was adhered to my skull. Studying the second image—a posterior view of my skull—I realized the tumor filled approximately a quarter of the area meant for my brain.

I began to cry.

Lew, who had been sitting in a chair on my left, rose and gently pulled the two pictures from me. He wrapped his fingers around mine, comforting me the best he could. From his expression, I knew he could not comprehend the news that had just assaulted us.

"Mrs. Luftig, can I get the hospital chaplain for you? A priest or maybe a pastor?"

Priest? Pastor? I don't need them, I need ...

"Dr. Modi," I said. "Are you a man of faith?"

The expression on his face changed from serious concern to peaceful reflection.

"Yes, as a matter of fact I am," he said smiling. "I called out to God a few months past. He was there, waiting for me." The doctor paused, as if remembering an earlier time.

He continued, "I know God well. That's why I asked if you'd prefer to share this news and pray with someone."

"Please, Dr. Modi, I'm not interested in finding a priest or hospital chaplain to pray with me. I want you to pray for me."

That was odd.

Here I lay in a hospital bed, facing the greatest fear I had ever known, and I asked the doctor, a man I'd met only a few hours earlier, to pray for me.

Sweet Presence

A profound sense of peace washed over my tiny, curtained ER room. With Lew and Dr. Modi on opposite sides of my bed, we reached out a free hand to one another. Uncertainty loomed. Yet an unmistakable, almost palpable, presence of God pressed in.

"Dear heavenly Father," I whispered. "Thank You for being the God above all gods. Thank You for the blessings You have bestowed on me today. I know the stars hang in the heavens because You put them there. You make the sun rise in the East. Your Word tells me that You knew me before I took form in my mother's belly[2] and even know the hairs on my head."[3]

Pausing, I took a breath and continued with timid confidence.

"Father, I know this tumor is no surprise to You. I know You have been aware of the day, hour, and moment I would have my seizure. I know You were even there in my bedroom when I thought I was dying."

Tears streamed my cheeks, yet I continued.

"I know what I know, Lord, but I have to say I've never been this afraid before. Have You forgotten me? Please help me." I squeezed Lew's hand. "Father, I'm afraid and confused. Please stay close. Amen."

After moments of silence and with a raspy voice, thick from holding back tears, Lew prayed.

"Heavenly Father, we love and honor You. Please, give me back my wife."

All he had was this one bold prayer. Yet in his shock, he still honored God.

"Dear God," Dr. Modi offered his part of our group prayer with a quiet voice. "Thank You for Your provisions that fill our day. I pray You bless Robin. Help her trust You through this process and after. Amen."

---

2   Jeremiah 1:5
3   Matthew 10:30

We let go of one another's grasp. I became cognizant of the voices and clamoring noises beyond the curtain. I could feel the sweet presence of God in the still air around us. A profound serenity washed over me. That's when I heard four words from deep in my heart. Words I had heard weeks earlier.

Do you trust Me?

In a flash, I recalled the moment in the car when I'd heard God speak those words.

Now, I may only have ten days until surgery ... less than two weeks to accomplish everything I hoped to accomplish, experience everything I yearned to experience, and say everything I wanted to say to those who needed to hear from me.

Though Dr. Modi deferred the responsibility of giving me a more in-depth assessment of my condition to the neurosurgeon, it was glaringly obvious he didn't say I'd be just fine. He gave no guarantee I would make it through surgery, let alone have a life beyond it. And if I did survive the surgery, there were no promises of what type of life I would lead.

Lew leaned over the padded bedrail to give me a kiss. His breath smelled of stale coffee. I must have been a bit pungent myself. Fear and adrenaline coated my skin. My tongue tried to wet my parched mouth. I had to be satisfied with ice chips. *I don't even have the luxury of smelling of stale coffee.*

It didn't matter. *Nothing really mattered. I may die soon.* I took in a deep breath and tried to focus.

In those early morning hours, my mind raced, seeking out the promises of God's trustworthiness. One thought stood front and center: *Do you trust Me?*

Memories of rich experiences throughout my life faded. This was the motherlode—my moment of truth.

I may only have ten days to live, and I needed to know if I believed God was trustworthy. Was my faith strong enough? Could I believe that His umbrella of protection would be enough to keep me safe from life's tragedies? From death? From being less than I was?

It's Just You and Me Now

Tragedy comes in many shapes and sizes. It can come in an instant or seep into your life like a slow, constant drip. Without warning, that drip turns to a tsunami, destroying everything in its path.

In the space at the end of this chapter, write about what happened to you. Get it on paper. If you need extra space, find more sheets and fold them in between these pages. Hold nothing back.

Fearful about being honest? Don't be. If necessary, hide this book from onlookers. If you seek God's best during your worst, you must express your worst situation in all its details. Secrets don't keep you safe, they keep you in bondage. Risk it. Trust that God is waiting with an umbrella to protect you from the elements you are experiencing.

Don't be polite or sugarcoat your words. Your worst—the tragedies that control a portion of your world—deserve an honest stare-down.

Take all the time you need. I'll wait.

UNDER THE UMBRELLA

Here's your chance. Empty your heart on this page. Write all you are feeling as well as what you're afraid to feel. Remember, it's for your eyes only.

_____

_____

_____

_____

_____

_____

_____

_____

_____

_____

_____

_____

_____

_____

_____

_____

_____

Chapter Two

Confusion

Journal entry: Saturday, April 2, 2011, 6:30 a.m.

The nurses checked me into Room 711. The ER staff scheduled me for a meeting with a neurosurgeon later today. They said another MRI was scheduled to map my brain for surgery.

Weekend plans are cancelled. All plans are put on hold for now. More pressing issues are at hand. Matters more important than the piddly ones that filled my thoughts just hours ago.

This whole experience is surreal.

*O*ften, tragedy takes us by surprise ... that's one of the reasons it's so tragic.

"Why is this happening?"

Lew held my hand but had no answers.

I called each of my children and listened to the shattering silence they offered when I told them I may only live a few more days.

Then they asked for reassurance. They wanted me to be fine. But I couldn't lie to them. I couldn't offer them hope beyond what I knew. I explained to each of them that there were no promises concerning my recovery. Their silence soon turned to sobs—sobs that pierced my heart.

Along with the pain that came from hearing my children's distress, confusion moved in and took up residence in me. Questions abounded.

If God is all-loving, how could this happen? What good can come from something so bad? Does God hate me?

The tragedies we face might differ, but they often conjure the same reactions. Confusion, disorientation, and incredible frustration. They may be hard to explain or wrap your mind around. How could something so devastating happen to your perfect life? Or maybe your life hasn't been perfect, but you've learned to work with any disfunction you experience. Can you relate to any of the following conundrums:

> You're faced with a divorce you never saw coming.
>
> You're facing cancer for the second time.
>
> Your child gets caught up with the wrong crowd.
>
> A life-long friend breaks a confidence.
>
> You were sexually abused as a child and can't carry the shame any longer.
>
> You lose your job.
>
> Or, like me ... you were told you had a brain tumor and may only have days to live.

While we often feel isolated and alone, it helps to see how others deal with similar reactions. Well-known Christian philosopher and author Nicolas Wolterstorff shared how his faith was stretched to its breaking point when his twenty-five-year-old son was killed in a mountain climbing accident. As he reflected over his agony and loss in *Lament for a Son*[1], he found he needed more than an answer to the question *Why?* He needed an affirmation of God's presence during his grief.

> "God is not only the God of the sufferers but the God who suffers .... It is said of God that no one can behold His face and live. I always thought this meant that no one could see His splendor and live. A friend said perhaps it meant that no one could see his sorrow and live. Or perhaps his sorrow is splendor. Instead of explaining our suffering, God shares it."

Scripture is full of stories of people who suffered heartache as well. Think of the prophet Elijah. He had fantastic success with stopping the rain and bringing a boy back from the dead (1 Kings 17). A few years later he even challenged Ahab to a pray-off that ended with Elijah winning the Mirror Ball Pray Off Trophy and killing 450 prophets of Baal and four hundred prophets of Asherah (1 Kings 18).

He was riding high; then King Ahab's wife Jezebel sent a message to Elijah telling him she would kill him before the day was over (1 Kings 19). *What?* This devastated Elijah to the point of wanting to die: "I have had enough, Lord. Let me die. I am no better than my ancestors" (1 Kings 19:4).

But don't miss the power of what happened next. After God sent angels to tend to him so he could rest, Elijah set off for Mount Sinai to see God—the same place that Moses had gone to meet with Him.

Elijah relied on what he knew, and he knew he needed to meet God, just as Moses had.

The New Testament offers stories of confusion as well. Think of Peter's response to Jesus when He asked His disciples if they were going to desert him like everyone else had, to which Peter replied, "Lord, to whom shall we go?" (John 6:68).

Watch for Warning Signs

While not all tragedies come with warning signs, some do. If warnings show up, be prepared to recognize them.

Looking back over my life, every negative situation I got myself into I now see came with warning signs I never heeded. It can be difficult to view ourselves objectively, but we need to strive to be independent thinkers.

Does something not seem right in your world? You can't put your finger on what's wrong. Seek an objective point of view from a trusted friend if necessary but be on guard for those who don't want the best for you. True friends can be objective and many times will have their own tests for validity. Still, while it's terrible to be fooled, it's worse to deal with the consequences of bad choices.

You can often catch warning signs you missed when you use hindsight. Maybe when a person *seems* stoic, they are not romantic or mysterious, but moody and self-absorbed. Or that first drink seemed harmless, but the fifth left you unable to drive unimpaired.

We all have made bad choices when we knew better. If only we had listened to our *Knower*—that voice inside that screams *Warning! Warning!*—when it tried to warn us of impending danger. It's awful to feel foolish or angry with ourselves when looking back to discover that we missed the obvious.

Marriage for example. Are conversations strained between the wife and husband? Does she choose to hang out with friends instead of being with her family? Does he make excuses to hang out with the new girl at work? Has the light jealousy that started out so sweet and protective early in their relationship turned possessive or violent?

Warning signs are a preface to a marriage about to see trouble.

Often, we approach our health without recognizing warning signs. Popping antacids because of indigestion instead of finding the root cause. Eating that third bowl of ice cream before bed, never connecting the excess with the nightmares or the high blood sugar or the weight gain. Ignoring the warning signs of extreme thirst or fatigue, hoping the signs will go away. Going to dinner with friends who happen to have a drink or two with dinner, knowing that while you don't drink often, when you do, you binge. *It's fun ... what's the harm?*

Beware. Warning signs are often there to alert us of lurking problems.

Plenty of negative behaviors seem to offer great short-term payoff but can cause devastation in your life. Do you exercise or monitor your food intake excessively? While you may be the talk of the office for having a svelte physique, a food obsession could be a real issue for you.

Don't disregard this book or get in the way of your *Knower*. Stop confusion in its tracks and pay attention to warning signs. If addressing uncomfortable topics seems a bit awkward, work through it.

If you're in the middle of a life tragedy, don't think I'm blaming you.

Be proactive. Be open to self-examination.

I'm a huge advocate for reflecting over each day before you go to sleep. Was it a good day? Were there moments that caused you to pause due to not understanding something? Often when we don't understand it's because what we *think* we see is not true. Did your vision fog over for no apparent reason? Make note of it. It may be nothing. But it also may be a warning of things to come.

Listening to your *Knower* or being open to unsettling changes around you could save years of conflict and pain.

When Warning Signs Don't Come

But what if there are no warning signs at all? How do you cut through the confusion when you're blindsided?

- ☑ When you receive that dreaded, unexpected call in the middle of the night ...
- ☑ Or a drunk driver hits your teenager coming home from school in the middle of the afternoon ...

☑ Or a violent storm wipes out your home and all your belongings ...

☑ Or a crazed shooter kills your friend along with several other people.

You hear the news and immediately become disoriented. Numb. Wrapped in disbelief. *This can't be happening!* Then reality hits. And you might want to die. All the loss floods your heart and mind.

Why would God allow this? What good can come from this? Can't He love me without hurting me? Would it have been too much to ask for Him to allow me some peace?

Whether you had warnings or were blindsided with catastrophe, confusion still runs rampant. How can loss make sense? We love God, and He says He loves us. Yet *this* happened?

Overcoming Confusion

Tragedies can shake our faith. It's easy to lose our way when darkness creeps in. It's easy to slip into a spiritual funk when confused. But the reality is this: being a Christian never guarantees a pain-free life. We still suffer loss.

No matter how much or how hard you pray, disease still hits. Storms still wipe out entire communities. People still get shot. Marriages still end. Friends still betray trusts.

Life still hurts.

Overcoming the funk that accompanies confusion starts with clarifying the situation. This needn't take a long period of time. It can happen in an instant, or it may take years. But finding clarification is vital.

When a marriage ends, tragedy and confusion envelop you, but as you reflect over your situation and gain clarity, you may be able to see your role in the demise of the marriage. At what point did that marriage stop being a priority? When did the attention and opinion of those outside the marriage become more important that one another's? Asking hard questions in no way excuses bad behavior, and now is not the time to assign blame. These are simply examples of questions you should ask when looking for clarity within confusion.

We also must seek wisdom in our confusion. Proverbs tells us, "For the Lord gives wisdom; from His mouth come knowledge and understanding" (Proverbs 2:6 NIV). This is a sin-laden world, not at all what God originally intended. When situations go beyond our ability, it's amazing what He can offer to us when we pray and seek His wisdom.

Wise counsel is also vital. Seek advice from a friend or professional or listen when wise counsel comes without solicitation. Wise counsel is also found in books. Two of my favorites about marriage are Gary Thomas' *Sacred Marriage: What If God Designed Marriage to Make Us Holy More Than to Make Us Happy?*[2] and Gary Chapman's, *The Five Love Languages: How to Express Heartfelt Commitment to Your Mate.*[3]

Tragedy can control everything around you, as expressed in the book *Sober Mercies.*[4] The book tells the story of Heather Harpham Kopp, an established editor in the Christian literary world—who was a closet drunk. Heather struggled to make sense of life as she tried to control her drinking. She considered her drinking as "it's just wine" until she realized she was hiding wine bottles in her boots in her closet and carrying tiny bottles in her purse for a quick pick-me-up. It was only after she gave herself over to the Source greater than herself that she found clarity.

Only outside intervention can break confusion's hold. God has sent the Holy Spirit to intervene for us. Listen to God's soft voice. He is speaking to you. Don't ignore Him.

Your Plans Could Use Some Help

Ever think your plans are better than God's? How many prayers have you offered that gave a three-point plan on how God was wrong? You see it in the Old Testament. When the oxen carrying the ark stumbled, Uzzah stopped it from falling by reaching out and steadying it. But because he touched the ark—something strictly forbidden by God—he died on the spot (2 Samuel 6). Or Aaron's sons Nadab and Abihu, when they wanted to glorify God. They chose and offered an ordinary fire—a fire not from the altar of God—in worship, and God's fire turned and consumed them right there on the spot. (Leviticus 10:1-2).

The New Testament apostles were forever coming up with better plans than what they thought Jesus had. Peter tried to protect Jesus when a guard came to arrest him (John 18:10-11). Jesus even labeled John and James as Sons of Thunder. We can see why in Luke 9, when the residents of a Samaritan village did not welcome them, and they asked Jesus, "Lord, do you want us to call fire down from heaven and destroy them?" (Luke 9:54 NIV).

They all thought they had better plans. But their plans did not meet with God's standards.

It's Time for You to Go to Work

When we clear confusion from our mind, we have a better chance to accept that life was never meant to be easy. It can be messy ... some times are messier than others. But when we find ourselves in a messy situation—or in a full-blown tragedy—our only option is to push through.

Pushing through can take work—lots of work.

Accept that God has a plan. Ask Him to reveal it to you. Take on the tenacity of Jacob and wrestle with God if needed (Genesis 32:22-32). Don't let go of Him until you have an answer. It may be hard ... *I mean really hard*. But it will be worth it. Steer away from clichés that have no substance. While soundbites like *God is my co-pilot,* or *the Bible says it and that settles it* make good bumper stickers, nothing matches the unwavering knowledge that comes from grappling with God for answers.

Think about how loving parents treat their children. When children don't understand, aren't they encouraged to ask questions, maybe even to push back a bit? To challenge what they've heard? Parents allow this because they know that's how people learn. And parents want their children to trust them enough that they can grow through the process.

God is like that. He's with us as we learn as well. Apostle Paul's words are very clear on this in 2 Corinthians 4: "We are hard pressed on every side, but not crushed; perplexed, but not in despair; persecuted, but not abandoned; struck down, but not destroyed" (2 Corinthians 4:8-9 NIV). God is with us through every moment.

And He's with you in your moment of need.

Now's your opportunity to focus your thoughts onto paper. Write all your feelings surrounding your situation. All of them. Don't edit the list or try to keep it cohesive. Just write.

Don't be surprised if your confusion brings you to untapped anger. Let it flow onto paper. Do you feel like using words you typically don't use? If it helps you express what is inside, use all the words you need. After you start, be willing to walk away from it for a bit. Take a nap. Have some lunch. Discovering your deepest thoughts rarely comes at one sitting. But make sure you return.

After you finish, review your list to make sure you haven't missed anything. It's very important to be honest—vigorously honest—with yourself. I can't overstress this part. Remember, keep your list private. These scribblings are only for you to see.

Once you feel like you're done, it's time to dive into Scripture. You may have your own favorites, but here are some of mine that pull me into a healing frame of mind:

"For nothing is impossible with God" (Luke 1:37 ESV).

"But Jesus looked at them and said, 'With man this is impossible, but with God all things are possible'" (Matthew 19:26 ESV).

"For God has not given us a spirit of fear, but of power and of love and of a sound mind" (2 Timothy 1:7 NKJV).

"I praise you, for I am fearfully and wonderfully made. Wonderful are your works; my soul knows it very well" (Psalm 139:14 ESV).

UNDER THE UMBRELLA

Do you feel exhausted? Then you're finished. Now it's time to tell God about it. In the last chapter, you wrote your feelings surrounding your worst situation. Now write your feelings about God's place in your life.

_____

_____

_____

_____

_____

_____

_____

_____

_____

_____

_____

_____

_____

_____

_____

_____

_____

Chapter Three

Doubt

Journal entry: Sunday, April 3, 2011, 3:00 a.m.

It's quiet now—hospital-room quiet. I'm glad Lew brought my Bible to me yesterday. Beginning the day with Scripture and prayer always helps.
I'm trying to stay focused and stay positive. But how can I stay positive when I'm dealing with so much unknown? I could die or, if I don't die, I could be an invalid—even catatonic. Is that what you want, God? I am so ready to wake from this terrible nightmare.

The Morning's Prayer of Uncertainty

Father, please help me get my head around what's happening to me. I'm not strong enough to go through this on my own. I'm scared. I don't think I have what it takes. Are you sure, Father? Is this really what you meant to happen? Lord, are you there?

*I*thought I had stopped doubting God when I finally surrendered my heart to Christ after years of resisting Him. Before, I thought I had everything figured out. But my life was a mess.

When I welcomed my Savior into my life, I was able to watch how that one choice turned my life from darkness to becoming a daughter of the King. I thought my shadowy days were finally behind me. I learned to reach beyond life's circumstances. God's love was enough. He repeatedly proved Himself faithful.

Faithful enough, anyway. That's how I saw it.

Yet, even with that knowledge and experience, lying in my hospital bed, I doubted God. All my earlier efforts had been to please Him. And for all my hard work, I got a mass on my brain.

That didn't make sense to me.

After confusion set in, doubt soon followed. And once doubt finds a home in your life, it's hard to kick out.

Doubt Has Been Around Forever

While doubt may be new to you, it's been around forever. And not just in the secular world—doubt was alive and well throughout Scripture. The serpent said to Eve in the Garden of Eden, "Did God really say, "You must not eat from any tree in the garden?" (Genesis 3:1 NIV). The authors of Job, Lamentations, Ecclesiastes, and Jeremiah all share stories of confusion and doubt. We can't forget David, a man after God's own heart, who is credited for writing some of the most beautiful psalms. Yet at times he doubted God's love: "How long, LORD? Will you forget me forever? How long will you hide your face from me?" (Psalm 13:1 NIV).

Seems crazy, right?

If scriptural heroes are too lofty for you, how about the doubting Christians of contemporary history? Charles Spurgeon (1834–1892),[5] one of history's celebrated preachers, shared in his sermon *The Desire of the Soul in Spiritual Darkness*:

> "I think, when a man says, 'I never doubt,' it is
> quite time for us to doubt him, it is quite time

for us to begin to say, 'Ah, poor soul, I am afraid you are not on the road at all, for if you were, you would see so many things in yourself, and so much glory in Christ more than you deserve, that you would be so much ashamed of yourself, as even to say, It is too good to be true.'"[6]

If Spurgeon is too far removed from your world, consider one of the all-time most beloved Christian authors and thinkers—and doubters—C.S. Lewis (1898–1963).[7] Lewis wrote:

"Faith, in the sense in which I am here using the word, is the art of holding on to things your reason has once accepted, in spite of your changing moods ... That is why faith is such a necessary virtue: unless you teach your moods 'where they get off,' you can never be either a sound Christian or even a sound atheist."[8]

And the world was rocked when the sainted Mother Teresa (1910–1997) shared laments in letters to her spiritual advisors:

"Darkness is such that I really do not see—neither with my mind nor with my reason—the place of God in my soul is blank—There is no God in me—when the pain of longing is so great—I just long and long for God ... Sometimes—I just hear my own heart cry out—'My God'—and nothing else. The torture and pain I can't explain."[9]

God doubters—all of them. Yet each one is remembered as a pillar of Christian faith. If doubt played such a dynamic part in the lives of these and other scriptural heavy-hitters, could doubt play a role—and then a purpose—in your life as well?

Is It Okay to Doubt God?

If life's trials are often where doubt begins, does that automatically mean doubts are bad?

Not necessarily.

When you follow the progression of doubt, you'll see it begins with a question (*Did God really say? ... How long, LORD? ... Will you forget me forever?*), then waits for a response.

It's in the response that doubt either dies or flourishes.

Flourishing Doubt

I started doubting God the moment after I met Him. When I was a child and accepted Christ as my savior[4], I felt a bit disappointed. *Shouldn't I feel different inside? Maybe appear a bit more angelic?* As one month rolled into another, I listened to my pastor's sermons and paid close attention to other Christians, attempting to figure out what it took to "do Christian." I heard their words and watched their actions, noting what I heard didn't always match what I saw. Some points matched, yet discrepancies often glared. I witnessed a disparity between what I experienced and what the Bible said.

My questions weren't the problem—children often spill over with questions—but they were enough to cause confusion, because the explanations were enveloped in dissonance. When I saw mix-matched theology, I should have asked for clarification. A wiser person would have asked.

But I didn't.

That's when doubt crept in. *Maybe God isn't real. Or, if He is real, maybe He's just not real for me.* The more I pondered, the more serious the questions became.

---

4   For clarification, I accepted Christ as my savior when I was a child, but he didn't become Lord of my life until I was an adult.

If God is in control like the pastor said, then why are there starving children in China?[5] Granted, my belly was full, yet there was news of a world that still struggled. My unaddressed doubt began to grow and fester. It didn't take long before I chose to rely on my own sensibility—because it made sense. And that train of thought said it was best to walk away from God.

You may have doubts of your own. You may be facing a tragedy. If left unattended, your doubts may affect your faith. Doubts may eventually open the door to pain and darkness.

In Philip Yancey's book *The Question That Never Goes Away*,[10] Yancy tells of the time in 2012 when he traveled to Yugoslavia, then on to Sarajevo, and saw where East and West met. On one side of the street were beautiful sidewalk cafes and onion-domed buildings, such as those found in Vienna. When he looked on the other side of the street, he was reminded of his travels to Istanbul and all its tea shops and spice markets. Women were walking around wearing their niqabs in Sarajevo just as they did in Istanbul. He writes:

> "From every corner of Sarajevo I heard ghostly echoes of the question that haunts human history: Why doesn't God intervene? Why not take out Hitler before he turned on the Jews? Why not rescue Sarajevo after four days, not four years? 'Ah, it is a strange world,' said one of the characters in Chaim Potok's *My Name is Asher Lew*. 'Sometimes I think the Master of the Universe has another world to take care of, and He neglects this world, God forbid.'"[11].

---

5   Growing up in the 1950s, the go-to tear-jerking anecdote was always about the starving children in China.

39

There's nothing wrong with doubt. Even the great minds, as noted earlier, suffer from it. But they don't stop existing. They either keep searching for the answer or find peace in the fact that the answer isn't for them to find.

Are There Consequences for Doubting God?

From the Old Testament through the New, you can find stories about people who doubted God. And if there were backlashes from doubting, you'd think we would have seen it. What we see, however, are consequences that didn't manifest in doubting, but as a result of the actions taken because of their doubt. God didn't punish Abraham and Sarah for their lack of belief regarding having children. Their problems came when they tried to control their situation by offering Sarah's maidservant to Abraham (Genesis 21:9-11). It wasn't the doubt that brought a backlash. It was their attempt to strip control from God that earned them consequences.

If God punished doubters in the New Testament, John the Baptist's words could have earned him a mighty smiting (Matthew 11:2-3). To paraphrase John's message to Jesus, *Are you the Messiah? If not, get out of my way so I can wait for the one who is.* Jesus didn't punish him for his declaration. He shouted His love for John to the crowd around Him (Matthew 11:7-14).

We see in Scripture how God not only blesses *when* someone doubts, but He blesses them *in* their doubts. Read the story of Gideon in Judges 6. While his doubt drove him to thresh his wheat in a wine press (v. 11), the Lord saw his value as a mighty warrior (v. 12) and someone who could lead Israel from the Midianites (v. 14). Gideon's response? No, not me (v. 15).

Yet God blessed him and gave him the strength he needed.

And what did Gideon do? He still needed confirmation from God.

> "'I will place a wool fleece on the threshing floor. If there is dew only on the fleece and all the ground is dry, then I will know that you will save Israel by

40

my hand, as you said.' And that is what happened. Gideon rose early the next day; he squeezed the fleece and wrung out the dew—a bowlful of water. Then Gideon said to God, 'Do not be angry with me. Let me make just one more request. Allow me one more test with the fleece, but this time make the fleece dry and let the ground be covered with dew.'" That night God did so. Only the fleece was dry; all the ground was covered with dew" (Judges 6: 37-40 NIV).

Doubt doesn't have to be a bad thing. It's how we handle it that matters.

Overcoming Doubt

Have you thrown this book across the room yet? If so, no worries. I've thrown a few books myself. This book is not a fixer, and your tragic situation may still loom. But your response to what you've read may be the beginning of a new way of looking at life. Are you stuck in this chapter? You may want to revisit Chapter Two and dig a bit deeper into why you can't move forward.[6] Take whatever time you need and re-read what you wrote.[7]

The times I doubted God most was when life moved in a direction I didn't choose. Like times when I had too much month and not enough money. Or when a perfect job I applied for went to someone else. Or when I was told I may only have ten more days to live.

My focus spotlighted loss.

---

6   I warned that you may need to walk away from it for a moment to gain an honest assessment of your true feelings.

7   If you thought this was going to be an easy beach read, you picked the wrong book. You are in the fight of your life. A fight to see beyond your pain and find what God has waiting for you. Don't give up!

And you. What are you doubting? Your marriage? Job choice? Whether life is worth living?

God knew we'd have a difficult time with doubt. I'm thankful for the gift found in James 1 that offers us a new view of calamity. The second verse begins the passage, "My brothers and sisters, you will have many kinds of trouble. But this gives you a reason to be happy" (James 1:2 NIV). If you'd prefer to hear from Jesus himself, "Go back and report to John what you hear and see: The blind receive sight, the lame walk, those who have leprosy are cleansed, the deaf hear, the dead are raised, and the good news is proclaimed to the poor" (Matthew 11:4-5 NIV).

To overcome doubt, we must reach beyond our circumstances to appreciate that He has a plan. Reflect over His presence in your life. See His past faithfulness. Why then wouldn't He be faithful now? If there is nothing you can see in your past to remind you of God's faithfulness, ponder over what you can rely on—God's promises. Here are a few:

"Never will I leave you; never will I forsake you"
(Hebrews 13:5 NIV).

"Because of the Lord's great love we are not consumed, for his compassions never fail. They are new every morning; great is your faithfulness" (Lamentations 3:22-23 NIV).

"Neither angels nor demons, neither the present nor the future, nor any powers, neither height nor depth, nor anything else in all creation, will be able to separate us from the love of God that is in Christ Jesus our Lord" (Romans 8:38-39 NIV).

Feelings of doubt have power when we allow them to rule. But the *knowledge* of Christ and His Word is everlasting. To get answers, you must ask the questions.

Why did this happen to me?

Know that God understands your pain and welcomes your questions, even if they come in the form of yells and rants. He yearns for your attention and prefers even the screaming over a relationship full of icy silence. David reminded God of his pain: "Record my misery; list my tears on your scroll—are they not in your record?" (Psalm 56:8 NIV).

We can remind Him of our pain too.

Need more proof that God wants to hear your woes? David cuts loose on Him in another Psalm, "Have mercy on me, Lord, for I am faint; heal me, Lord, for my bones are in agony. My soul is in deep anguish. How long, Lord, how long? ... I am worn out from my groaning. All night long I flood my bed with weeping and drench my couch with tears. My eyes grow weak with sorrow; they fail because of all my foes" (Psalm 6:3, 6-7).

Doubt can be a killer, but it doesn't have to be. Choose to focus on what is true: God loves you and He's right there with you. He's with you now. Share your doubts. He's big ... He can handle it.

UNDER THE UMBRELLA

Do you feel like a bad Christian when you doubt God? How do you think God wants you to feel right now?

_____

_____

_____

_____

_____

_____

_____

_____

_____

_____

_____

_____

_____

_____

_____

_____

_____

Chapter Four

Focus

The Morning's Prayer of Uncertainty

Father I have never been more confused than now. What am I missing? The doctors said I didn't do anything that caused this tumor. My head knows it's true, but my heart is unsettled. Why did You bring me out of so much darkness only to take everything away? How can this be good? How can my brain tumor bring You glory? I know You're omniscient and all, but I can't conceive why this is happening. What am I supposed to do now?

*M*onday after my diagnosis, I contacted my employer with the news. They placed me on immediate leave under the Family and Medical Leave Act (FMLA). This freed up my time to focus on the medical attention I needed. It also gave me comfort knowing my position would be held and waiting for me. Lew's employer graciously gave him permission to telecommute for his job, allowing him to be home as well. He was there to help when I needed to meet with doctors as well as offer comfort and assure my safety.

Over breakfast, Lew and I put pen to paper and began to set priorities. We had five business days to work with and no do-overs. We needed to make arrangements for all possible outcomes. These lists became vital. I needed to stay focused.

Horses or Zebras?

"Life is changing. I'm already forgetting stuff." I rubbed my clenched hands together, wondering whether I was cold or just dealing with a fresh case of nerves. Lew, ever-present, offered wisdom.

"Hearing hoofbeats behind you doesn't mean they're from zebras, Robin."

"*Wha?*"

He put down his pen and smiled at me. "Okay, so you're forgetful. Don't automatically think it's the tumor. It's just like when you're on the road and you hear hooves behind you, it's probably just a plain horse, not an exotic zebra from Africa." His grin widened a bit. "We're in Pennsylvania, Robs, remember?"

Lew held his fingers up as he counted. "One, they put you on lots of medication. Maybe that's why you're forgetting. Two, you're sleep deprived. That could be another reason. Three, you had a massive seizure a few days ago. Your body may still be healing. Four, it may be a combination of things, or maybe something completely different."

He walked over and pulled my chair toward him, then knelt before me.

"It *could* be the tumor, Robs, but maybe you don't remember because of something else. Let's focus ... stick with what we know for sure."

Rely on What You Know

When death, a tragic diagnosis, or a betrayal from a loved one arrive without warning, our minds often turn to the question *Why?* Thoughts, often rooted in fear, run wild, giving our problems complete control. However, when we focus on what we *know* instead of what we *fear*, our confusion lessens.

We need to do our best to ponder on Truth and the God who wrote it. Pause and consider a few names for God, the author of Truth:

> *Jehovah Raah* translates to "The Lord is My Shepherd."

> *El Shaddai*[8] translates to "God Almighty."

> *El Roi* translates to "the God Who Sees Me."

> *Jehovah Rapha* translates to "the God Who Heals."

Let those names bounce around in your head for a moment. Your Almighty Shepherd ... who sees you right now ... wants you to be whole.

---

8   When I hear Amy Grant sing El Shaddai, I weep with gratitude. If you haven't heard it, give it a listen: https://www.youtube.com/watch?v=DuX-B1a3NBCw.

How to Focus

Need to see focus in action? It's everywhere. Watch any sports event on television, and you'll see players block out all distractions and only focus on the prize. Anyone who watched the 1996 Olympics gymnastics events will remember the focus and determination of Kerri Strug. We all sat on the edge of our seat[9] and watched this teenage girl with two torn ligaments in her foot push through the pain and execute a vault with unwavering power ... and focus. Through her pain, she was able to help the U.S. team finally win the gold medal in gymnastics.

Scripture also urges us to be focused. King Solomon, the wisest man of the Old Testament, shared much of his wisdom through the Book of Proverbs. He wrote, "Go to the ant ... watch and think about her ways, and be wise. She has no leader, head or ruler, but she gets her food ready in the summer, and gathers her food at the right time" (Proverbs 6:6-8 NLT). Even ants know the importance of focus.

Wisdom can be found throughout the New Testament as well. The Apostle Matthew wrote, "Watch! You do not know on what day your Lord is coming" (Matthew 24:42 NLT). Focus on God, not what is around you.

What to Do When You Receive Troubling News

It's difficult to prepare for the worst when you're in the middle of it. Find solace in the fact that all you can do is the next right thing.

Right now. This very second. You're reading this book. That's the best thing for you to do. Focus on the chapters. Ponder the scriptures. Don't let your mind wander.

Take a breath. Don't overanalyze your situation. Like Kerri Strug looking for an Olympic gold medal or an ant preparing for winter. We must look for the next right thing to do—then do it.

_____Let me share a secret with you. Even now, when I hear

9   Yes, I'm an oldster, but watch this for yourself. You'll see how focus can be so powerful. https://www.youtube.com/watch?v=O4um3YEX51k

devastating news, my natural instincts are to go into full-bore panic mode. Surprised? Don't be. Fighting "what-if-isms" is one of my greatest flaws. I struggle almost daily, worrying about what could happen. But seeing how others fought their what-if-isms gives me strength.

Victor Frankl, a survivor of the Theresienstadt, Auschwitz, Kaufering, and Türkheim concentration camps, overcame his life's worst situations and founded logotherapy, a school of psychotherapy.[10] In 1946, he wrote *Man's Search for Meaning*, chronicling his experiences as a camp inmate. According to Frankl, our response to unavoidable suffering is one of the principal ways to find our life's meaning.

> "Despair is suffering without meaning, he wrote, and everything can be taken from a man but one thing: the last of the human freedoms—to choose one's attitude in any given set of circumstances."[12]

When Possible, Be Proactive

How does anyone plan for the unexpected? What can we do to prepare for the unimaginable? How can we be proactive when facing unknowns?

By remembering that bad will happen.

Bad may be happening to you right now. And when you find you need more—maybe more tolerance and a deeper faith—refocus on God and not what's happening around you. You will once again gain what you need, along with a confidence that this tragedy will somehow come to an end.

Prepare Your Heart

Not all catastrophes are physical. Many include matters of the heart. While it's easy to see the need for help with a physical need, it's also important to know you will need attention if your disaster concerns the heart.

10   Logotherapy, a form of existential analysis practiced in the "Third Viennese School of Psychotherapy."

Be willing to risk and share your pain with a trusted friend. A good friend loves you and will cry along while you shed your tears. They will eat ice cream with you and are often available at the drop of a hat during bad times. And they will tell you the truth—that's what makes them a good friend.

If you're a member of a Bible study, consider opening up to them about your fears. Share your pain. If you've been a member of the group for any length of time, these people already know and love you. They may offer valuable insight. I use a personal caution when sharing with a group: women should share with women and men should confide in men. When emotions are running at a high speed, the enemy has a chance to slip in and cause confusion.

Talk to a trusted church leader. Often ministers are trained to find answers in Scripture. They also understand the importance of confidentiality. Sharing the thoughts that weigh on your heart can be a true source of comfort.

Depending on your situation, it may be wise to find a Christian counselor or psychologist who can help you maneuver your minefield. Many accept insurance coverage or have sliding scale rates for those without insurance. These professionals are able to assist you through this season. They are also objective and set apart from the situation itself. This distance enables them to see what you're dealing with impartially and objectively.

But no matter who you talk with, you must focus and prepare yourself. Whichever way you choose to focus on healing, make sure you include the following:

1. Recall memories of God's faithfulness.
2. Accept that God knows what He's doing.
3. Trust God's plan.
4. Anticipate God's favor.

Satan is thrilled when we lose focus and forget God's faithfulness from the past. He does cartwheels when we question if God—

or His plan for us—is enough. Count on it. The foundation of your beliefs will be tested during this time. To get through this challenge, you must know where to find strength. You must move from wanting to know ... to *knowing*.

Dive into Scripture. Find your favorites. Read them. Re-read them. Memorize them. I promise, the time will come when you are stretched to your breaking point and these verses may mean the difference between emotional survival and spiritual destruction. Don't try to fight the battle for your soul alone. It's a spiritual battle, and it belongs to God anyway. Be very clear that Satan wants to use you like a pawn. He doesn't care about you. What he wants to do is take you down—and all other Christ followers that he can.

Ephesians 6 warns us about taking on battles we are not designed to fight or win: "For our struggle is not against flesh and blood, but against the rulers, against the authorities, against the powers of this dark world and against the spiritual forces of evil in the heavenly realms. Therefore, put on the full armor of God, so that when the day of evil comes, you may be able to stand your ground, and after you have done everything, to stand" (Ephesians 6: 12-13 NIV, Emphasis Mine).

We're Not in This Alone

God never promised us an easy life. But He did tell us He'd always be with us. Apostle Paul wrote in 1 Corinthians 10:13: "Every test that you have experienced is the kind that normally comes to people. But God keeps his promise, and he will not allow you to be tested beyond your power to remain firm; at the time you are put to the test, he will give you the strength to endure it, and so provide you with a way out" (GNB).

Read books written by God-fearing men and women. These are great tools when trying to focus. Maybe your time to focus is the quiet time during your commute to and from work. Audible books are perfect for driving or while riding mass transportation. If you ride the bus or subway, put your earbuds in and focus on the words. If you need extra time, consider leaving for your job early and spending time there in prayer and devotion. This will not only help set the day on the right track, but it will cement the habit of turning to God at the beginning of each day.

During the spring of 2011, before my seizure, I enjoyed my car time listening to authors Steven Furtick[13] and Andy Stanley.[14] They brought God's promises alive. I came to understand that if God could work with Joshua and make the sun stand still for a full day, why couldn't He ride with me on my way home from work? And with God offering grace to someone like me, I wanted to learn about it—to revel in that grace.

Find what works for you when you need help with focusing your mind on godly influences. For me, it was the privacy of my car, Mondays through Fridays. I'm thankful I used that time. I had no idea God was preparing me for a brain tumor tragedy. You might need music to calm your heart. Or maybe having people around is important to you. Whatever it is, don't allow anyone or anything to *distract you* from your hurt. These tools need to help you focus on what God is trying to tell you.

How to Own Preparation

I said it earlier, but it needs to be repeated: *Find solace in the fact that all you can do is the next right thing.* It's difficult to prepare for the worst when you're in the middle of it. But knowing the right thing to do is vital.

Don't rely on your memory. Tragedy will strip it clean. Make notes of what you need to do. Put your needs on the next page or jot them on your phone. Anywhere you can revisit them and ponder. Remember how you read about the wisdom found in Scripture a few pages earlier? This is when you put that practice into action. Find at least four verses or Bible passages and keep them with you in your journal or on your phone. Anywhere you can readily get to them. Look at them. Remind yourself that you're not out of God's loving hand.

You will find that the more you focus on God, the less you think about your crisis. Yes, the problem is still there, and yes, it has rocked your world. But the problem, no matter how big, doesn't need to own you.

Focus!

You'll soon trust the process.

UNDER THE UMBRELLA

Revisit the four actions listed earlier in the chapter (Recall, Accept, Trust, and Anticipate) and write a plan to incorporate them in your focusing process.

_____

_____

_____

_____

_____

_____

_____

_____

_____

_____

_____

_____

_____

_____

_____

_____

_____

_____

Chapter Five

Trust

Journal entry: Tuesday, April 5, 2011, 12:02 p.m.

My list for my surgeon continues to grow—from serious (Exactly how bad can this be?) to frivolous (When will I be able to color my hair again after surgery?). Putting thoughts and feelings on paper pulls them into focus— crystallizing good thoughts while weakening the dark ones. Stay focused. It's the only chance I have to get beyond whatever is destined for me.

The Morning's Prayer of Uncertainty

My time is passing too quickly, Father. There are too many people I'm not going to be able to reach. God, I want to trust You; I'm trying to trust You. Father ... Are you there?

*B*reaking it down," I told Lew as we got ready for bed, "I have about 100 hours until surgery. I'm still struggling to get my head around all this. How do I? How do my kids? They loved me through a lifetime of mess-ups. Now I feel like I'm more spiritually and emotionally grounded ... and I *still* may have to leave them because of this stupid tumor."

Climbing under the covers for the night felt cozy, but because of the medication the doctors had prescribed, sleep escaped me. Hours passed as I lay in bed awake, my mind racing with dark thoughts and my heart too full of feelings. While I wanted to experience every possible waking moment, it didn't mean Lew needed to be awake too. I crawled out of bed, hoping not to interrupt his sleep.

Often, stressful times bring sleepless nights and dark thoughts. God's role in our lives may be questioned. Does He even exist? If so, how could He care about us? For me, facing the real possibility of death up close and personal put a fresh face on questions regarding God's presence. Does He know me—or even care?

Scripture gives us a resounding *Yes!*

In Psalm 139, King David sings of God's immeasurable love for us:

> "You know when I sit and when I rise; you perceive
> my thoughts from afar. You discern my going out
> and my lying down; you are familiar with all my
> ways"(v. 2).

Buried in Your Knower

It's a part of who you are: your *Knower*. It's where truth lives. Some people trust their *Knower* more than others. But we all have one.

A powerful story that gives me chills about a *Knower* is in the third chapter of Daniel and the story of Shadrach, Meshach, and Abednego. These three young men were going to be thrown into a fiery furnace because they would not denounce God and bow down to King Nebuchadnezzar:[11]

> "We know our God can save us, but if he chooses
> not to, he is still worthy to be praised."[15]

Study this story. They knew they could trust God's truth would triumph over facts. They were willing to risk their lives over it: "If we are thrown into the blazing furnace, the God we serve is able to deliver us from it, and he will deliver us from Your Majesty's hand. But even if he does not, we want you to know, Your Majesty, that we will not serve your gods or worship the image of gold you have set up" (v 17-18 NIV).

Check out King Nebuchadnezzar's facts:

- ☑ *Fact* – King Nebuchadnezzar said everyone was to bow down or die (vv. 5-6).
- ☑ *Fact* – Shadrach, Meshach, and Abednego did not bow down (v. 12).
- ☑ *Fact* – King Nebuchadnezzar was angry but gave them a second chance (vv. 13-15).
- ☑ *Fact* – King Nebuchadnezzar ordered a giant fire to be built (v. 19).
- ☑ *Fact* – King Nebuchadnezzar ordered the teens bound and thrown into the fire (v. 21).
- ☑ *Fact* – The fire was so hot that people near the fire died from its heat (v. 22).
- ☑ *Fact* – King Nebuchadnezzar was astonished when he looked in the fire and saw four men walking around (v. 25).
- ☑ *Fact* – King Nebuchadnezzar called to the teens, and when they came out, not a hair was singed nor did they smell of smoke (v. 27).

---

11   Who can say the Old Testament is boring after reading this story?

☑ *Fact* – Shadrach, Meshach, and Abednego's faith changed the hard heart of King Nebuchadnezzar, and he praised God (vv. 28-29).

King Nebuchadnezzar had facts on his side. But the faith of three young men changed the outcome around those facts.

I am not suggesting to ignore facts, but know you can claim the truths found in Scripture when you doubt God's trustworthiness.

During my worst, I had to believe that God was big enough to heal my brain, *but if He chose not to*, He was still worthy to be praised.

How big do you need God to be right now? To get the full essence of who God is, you may need to lean in a bit and get to know Him more personally.

A great lesson on leaning in to trust God is in the Old Testament book Habakkuk.[12] Here, we read a conversation, initiated by the Prophet Habakkuk, between him and God. Habakkuk is full of questions about the plight of the nation of Judah.

This three-chapter book is rich, showing a personal relationship between the prophet and the Lord. Habakkuk asks his questions— good questions—of God about how He could allow such evil to prosper. What does God do? He tells Habakkuk, "You haven't seen anything yet. It's going to get worse!"[16]

What we are dealing with may get worse.

Spiritual Maturity

In the last chapter, you read about focusing and preparation. Getting ready to deal with your worst takes more than just going to church on Sundays or raising your hands when singing contemporary worship songs. It can mean pressing through the pain, hoping that it will be over sooner than later. But truly trusting that one day it will be over.

Habakkuk shows us a pure version of praise and worship that he used to focus and prepare. He models for us a true trust—an

---

12   The word Habakkuk means "to embrace."

intimacy that comes from a solid relationship. It didn't come from what he *did*; it came from who he *was*. And he was an honoring friend of God.

You may ask, *Why do I have to think about honoring God right now? I'm really hurting!* I can relate. But in times of deep trouble, please consider that we need to think about God more than ever ... because maybe He's all we can count on at that moment. This process builds spiritual maturity.

We all need to strive for spiritual maturity when facing tragedy, and that maturity begins with trusting God. It's difficult to accept or desire spiritual maturity, because most of the time it comes from a challenge that makes us stretch. Sometimes it stretches everything we have—our knowledge, possessions, and our emotions. Because it can be painful, it hurts to even write about it.

In Dan Reiland's article *Is Spiritual Maturity an Impossible Road?*,[17] he explains that spiritual maturity has three components: spiritual intimacy, biblical knowledge, and holy obedience. All three are needed. If any one is missing, we run the risk of missing the blessings God yearns to give us.

The first leg of the spiritual maturity stool is spiritual intimacy—experiencing a relationship with God. It involves our heart as well as having a continual dialogue with Him. God created us as relational beings and wants a relationship with us. But it needs to be supported by the other aspects of spiritual maturity as well. Spiritual intimacy without biblical knowledge and holy obedience becomes *emotionalism*—the tendency to react emotionally or with undue indulgence or display of emotion.

Biblical knowledge involves the mind and is knowing the truth of God. But be careful. Biblical knowledge alone can turn the mildest person into a tyrannical Pharisee. Biblical knowledge without spiritual intimacy and holy obedience becomes *intellectualism*—the devotion to the exercise of intellect or to intellectual pursuits. Without biblical knowledge, we run the risk of engaging in self-importance.

The third leg of spiritual maturity is holy obedience. Holy obedience involves the will, which includes surrendering to the ways of God. Without spiritual intimacy and biblical knowledge, obedience becomes *legalism*—rules for rules' sake. Self-righteousness. Not at all what God is about.

God wants a relationship with us. A personal one, not stuffy or extra polite. We all have that relative ... the one who is a bit different than the rest of the family? When you finally force yourself to talk with this person at the family reunion, you only do it because your parents are watching. *God doesn't want to know you like that!* He wants you to feel comfortable to reach out to Him as a child would. Arms extended for Him to pick you up and hold you safely.

When dark clouds cover our path, spiritual maturity offers the light that will bring us through. When tragedy hits, we may falter, but we will not break. Our mind will instinctively seek God through prayer and His Word. When we are spiritually mature, our *spirit* reaches for the comforting words of God we hear and read, our *mind* reflects on biblical truth, and our *will* follows what His Truth has told us.

What if We Don't Hear from God?

"I want to trust God, but I don't know how."

Many people want to trust God. They want to believe that He loves them, but religion may have gotten in the way of a relationship with Him. Too many times, religion trumped relationship.

There. I said it. Called out the elephant in the room. We sometimes don't trust God because of a time when Christians messed everything up. Maybe it was their pharisaical attitude or one too many clichés offered that dealt you a terrible blow. Don't let anyone steal the joy God has waiting for you, even during this worst time of your life. If they're not willing to offer empathy and see life as you are experiencing it, you may need to filter their words to protect your heart.

Sometimes pain runs too deep for others to imagine. Understanding is the key.

"Where was God when I was being molested? I cried out to him but didn't hear a thing."

"I was just diagnosed with cancer the second time. Why would God allow this?"

"My husband lost his job, and we're sixty days from living on the street. We thought we did everything right. Is this how he treats his children?"

When we turn to our church family during times of trouble and receive glib one-liners, it's no wonder we turn away from God.

It went the same with Job, a blameless and honorable man (Job 1:2). After losing all of his children, property, and wealth, instead of blaming God, he praised Him (1:21). His luck stayed constant when his wife offered counsel ("curse God and die" Job 2:9). Then his friends came by to cheer him up. Instead, all they did was question what he had done to deserve this treatment from God (Job 4:7).

Don't forget the blind man Jesus healed. Even the disciples asked what sin caused this man to be blind (John 9:1-2).

God sees you in your tragedy. If He has not spoken to you about it, continue to listen.

Depths of Trust

Trust is fundamental. We have it from birth. Infants trust that someone will care for them with food and comfort. As we grow from infant ... to child ... to adolescent ... and into and through adulthood, we often forego depths of trust for independence. As we learn to care for ourselves, such as feed ourselves or cross the street safely, trust loses its all-encompassing power. We move from complete trust to selective trust. We begin offering trust to an attentive parent, teacher, or best friend. While our need for trust changes from fundamental to selective, its importance never does.

Write about those you have trusted most in your life.

As a child? _____

Why?

_____

_____

As a teen? _____

Why?

_____

_____

As an adult? _____

Why?

_____

_____

My who in all these categories was my dad. He was my hero, and I was his best girl. Our bond was always special. It wasn't unusual for him to pat the top of my head when I was a child or squeeze my hand when I was a teen.

"Love you, brat."

"Love you too, old man"

What he gave me was love—and a place for me to put trust.

As a single father, he even addressed some of those "difficult" conversations usually shared between mothers and daughters: unwed pregnancy, hormones, and periods.

We were able to have these chats because we invested time with one another. I knew if I didn't hear his voice right away, I could wait. He'd always come back and share his insight. It was from that relationship that I learned to talk to my heavenly father.

Trusting God

German poet Rainer Maria Rilke wrote,

> "Were it possible, we might look beyond the reach of our knowing ... Then perhaps we would endure our griefs with even greater trust than our joys. For they are the moments when something new has entered into us, something unfamiliar ... Everything within us steps back, a silence ensues, and something new ... stands in the center and is silent."[18]

I learned how to trust God through my relationship with my earthly father. Unfortunately, that's not the case for everyone, which often leaves a void.

So how do we trust a void? Well ... we can't. A surrogate is needed. Be it an uncle, trusted friend, pastor, or counselor. While a loving father is best, a trusted father figure—someone who understands and takes his responsibility seriously—can be used by God.

But God is always there to offer words of comfort. An Old Testament example is of King David—flawed as he was—as he offers insight on how to experience an authentic relationship with the universe's Creator. And God recognized David as a man after His own heart.[19]

Yet we struggle.

If you were not fortunate to have a relationship like I did with my earthly father, broaden your scope and see who you could trust. Revisit the list I asked you to write earlier in the chapter. Were you able to fill in the lines? If not, go back and try again.

This is important. Come back here when you have them.

From that list, who did you trust to hold your secrets?

Who offered you the most sound advice?

Who did you cry with and were not ashamed to show your tears?

We all need a point of reference on how and who to trust. If this chapter causes you to stumble a bit, don't move on. Stay here and recall someone trustworthy. If after considering it you still don't come up with person, ask a friend.

If you think enough of that person to discuss trustworthiness with them, maybe *that* person could be your point of reference.

When Trust is Tested

Sometimes our faith is tested until we can't see anything beyond our pain. But we must know that God sees us there. Even if we don't see Him, His love is still constant (Romans 8:38).

God's love for us is not contingent on anything. His love is continuous. You can trust in that. Jesus said, if we have faith the size of a mustard seed, we can move mountains (Matthew 17:20). When we find our faith is tested to the limits, that's when we need to clear away doubt and confusion and double down, focusing on what we know is truth. That's what Shadrach, Meshach, and Abednego did.

> "We believe our God can save us" (Daniel 3:17).
> "We believe our God will save us" (Daniel 3:17).
> "But even if He doesn't, we still believe and will praise our God" (Daniel 3:18).[my paraphrase]

Unbearable circumstances require extreme faith. The faith doesn't have to be big, but it must be unwavering. Sometimes you need the faith of three teenage boys named Shadrach, Meshach, and Abednego.

What Do You Do Now?

You may be up to your chin in problems, yet I ask you to trust God.

Oh, I can hear you now.

1)   *"Who is she kidding?"*

2)   *"She doesn't have a clue what's going on in my life right now."*

3)   *"It's not that easy."*

My answers to you are 1) nobody; 2) you're right; and 3) no one said it was going to be easy.

Satan delights in distracting you while you are facing troubles—with a voracity like you've never seen before. Don't let his sleight of hand trick you. You have unshakeable truths to fall back on. At the end of Chapter One, I asked you to lay it all out. If you need to go back and add that you don't trust God, do it now. At the end of Chapter Two, I asked you to write where you see God at work in your life. Big sightings and little sightings, you were to list all you could see. Now go back to your list. Examine it and add to that list if you need. As you move deeper into this book, you may remember more of God's handiwork. At the end of Chapter Three you wrote about what you thought God wanted you to feel, even when you doubted Him. You were to write with complete honestly. Revisit that list as well. Do you trust God enough to add to that list too? Or maybe you need to start over because you wrote what you thought the right answers were. If that's the case, this time write the *real* answers.

Remember, the process of finding your way out of your worst situation may take more time than you anticipated. But you can do this. Focus on what you know. Rely on your *Knower*. Get into your favorite Bible verses. Talk to God, and tell Him what you're dealing with. See how one chapter builds on the other.

You're doing great. Can you sense your trust building?

UNDER THE UMBRELLA

How can you focus on God's desires for you when nothing seems good? How can you trust His plans?

_____

_____

_____

_____

_____

_____

_____

_____

_____

_____

_____

_____

_____

_____

_____

_____

Chapter Six

Heartache

Journal entry: Wednesday, April 6, 2011, 11:27 p.m.

Today has been difficult.
Monday's surgery is near. Every day brings me closer
to more unknowns. The prognosis of this operation is a
relatively good one, and if I play the numbers, all will
be fine. But when I hear the stillness of the night and all
I have around me are my thoughts and my soul aches.
I need to rely on more than good numbers. Lord,
help me remember: God's purpose wins over my
inconvenience—even if that inconvenience means
my death.
There's so much I don't understand. God, please
don't leave me now.

The Morning's Prayer of Uncertainty

Why me, Father? Can't I be allowed to stay in a
good place for more than a breath of time? I try not to

listen to Satan's lies, but they scare me. I'm reaching for
you in my transparency, Father. My head knows Your
truth, but my heart wants to chuck it all. Can I trust
You to offer me mercy this one more time?

*I*feel helpless," I said, while having breakfast with Lew. "I feel
fine, but I know I'm sick—really sick. I could use my time at
home to work on a project. Maybe refinish that table I've been
putting off or start painting the spare bedroom. But everything is
put on hold. All I can do is wait until Monday."

"We're not in control here, Robs." I knew Lew was right. But
my heart still ached.

Whispering, I confessed. "Truth be told, honey, I don't know
if I can do this."

"You can," he reached for my hand and gave it a squeeze. "And
you can do more. I have faith in you. And in God." He smiled. "I
trust you both."

Lew's words soothed my soul. He trusted me, maybe more
than I deserved.

The Dreaded Question ... Why?

Dealing with a ginormous hurt can expose you to a level of
emotions you've never dealt with before. As I did with my brain
tumor experiences, you've found yourself in the midst of adversity.
And with adversity comes heartache.

Unfortunately, we need adversities in our lives. They give life
depth. The saying, "all sunshine makes a desert" rings true. Watch
any movie or read any good novel and you'll find adversity and
heartache. Granted, it's not what we want for ourselves in the
moment. We don't choose a life with conflict. We want our lives
to come straight from a place of perfection. If we were completely
honest, we'd prefer to watch others deal with their heartache so we
can learn from their experiences. Right?

But it doesn't work that way. To fully appreciate—in our human
and limited ability—how strong God's love for you is, you need to

experience all the heartache and adversity firsthand.

As you've grown after reading the previous chapters of this book,[13] you've tackled focusing onto truth. That's the good news.

The bad news is ... the problem still exists. And so does heartache.

C. S. Lewis tells us in *The Problem of Pain* that "All suffering is suffering. There's no such thing as 'the sum of the world's suffering.' There are simply individual people who hurt. And who wonder why God permits it."[20]

Consider Mary watching her son Jesus die on the cross. I cannot imagine any greater heartache. She watched her son—a perfect man, yet, her baby boy—take in His last breath as He died for sins that weren't His own.

That was the heartache over a perfect man. But what about the heartache over one not so perfect? Marie Monville faced that reality in the fall of 2006 when her then-husband, Charles Roberts, barricaded himself in an Amish schoolhouse in Lancaster County, Pennsylvania and gunned down one schoolgirl after another until ten little girls were shot, leaving five dead. Then he committed suicide. Marie tells of her horrific fight to save her faith in her book *One Light Still Shines: My Life Beyond the Shadow of the Amish Schoolhouse Shooting*.[21] When she received the phone call from her husband the morning of October 2, 2006, it marked the end of the life she knew, never to be the same.

> "Charlie, what's going on?" My entire body was suddenly alert, my heart racing and my hands trembling.
>
> "I'm not coming home."
>
> Have you ever felt a depth of cold so bitter it leaves you feeling hypothermic—stunning your soul, leaving your body shivering in confusion?

---

13   Don't try to skip ahead. It isn't the destination that brings healing ... it's the journey.

In such a moment, the heart has little time to contemplate or question; it's struggling merely to grasp the devastation ...

"What are you talking about?" I said. "What do you mean you aren't coming home?"

There was something he needed to do, he said. Something he should've taken care of a long time ago, and he was going to do it today ... Most of the things he said in our brief conversation made no sense. Why wasn't he coming home? Then he told me the police were already there—but I had no idea where there was.[22]

Marie's nightmare continued.

"I left a letter for you," he said. "It's on the top of the dresser, under a magazine. I'm sorry it has to be this way, Marie."

Consider the heartache as later that day the world watched on while one television station after another talked about the monstrous act the father of her children had committed hours earlier.

Days turned into weeks as Marie's nightmare continued. Doing her best to shield her children from the horrors in Pennsylvania, she was happy to accept a gift for the family to take a southern cruise over Christmas break. As she and her children arrived at the dock and waited in line to check in, a cruise-line crew member noticed they were from Pennsylvania and asked, "Do you live near where that Amish schoolhouse shooting happened?"[23] There was no escape for Marie. And as she learned, there are some heartaches that can only be carried by God.

Why Does God Permit So Much Pain?

Scriptures abound with heartache. Yet, over the years, the Bible has been said to be the greatest love story ever told. So why the dichotomy?

Or is it?

We all know life is full of changes, and most of the time they can be exciting. But nobody ever imagines that around a given corner, a crisis not of their making could be waiting to greet them.

Such a thing happened to Abigail in 1 Samuel 25. Abigail, a beautiful and intelligent woman, was married to a rich man named Nabal,[14] who was brutish and mean. David and his army were traveling through the wilderness of Maon, Nabal's back yard, and sent a few of his men to ask Nabal—ever-so-nicely—if he would consider sharing some of his feast with David and his men, since they had protected Nabal's flocks of sheep.

Nabal, in his barbaric fashion, said, "Who is this fellow David? Who does this son of Jesse think he is? There are lots of servants these days who run away from their masters. Should I take my bread and my water and my meat that I've slaughtered for my shearers and give it to a gang who comes from God knows where?" (1 Samuel 25:10-11).

When David heard the news, he went ballistic and was ready for a battle (v. 13).

In the meantime, one of Nabal's men told his wife Abigail about what transpired between his master and David's men. Abigail knew this meant trouble.

She flew into action and loaded donkeys with food and headed out to see David. Upon seeing him, she quickly dismounted her ride and bowed low before him (vv. 18-19, 23). She greeted David with great humility and took upon herself all the blame for her husband's foolishness. She offered David gifts of food and wine for him and his men (vv. 27). In return, David, who had been on the way to Nabal's house, spared Abigail's fool of a husband and all his servants from death (vv. 32-34). Abigail's heartache would come later, however, when Nabal died. But her heartache was short lived. Her life would later take a turn she never imagined (vv. 40-42).

---

14   Translated "fool."

Seeing life spring from the death of a dream is woven through the New Testament. Ponder this verse from John 12: "Truly, truly, I say to you, unless a grain of wheat falls into the earth and dies, it remains alone; but if it dies, it bears much fruit" (John 12:24 ESV).

Sometimes we have to watch a dream die to make room for another one—often greater than the previous. When we see plans fall apart, we often presume it's because of God's absence or lack of concern. Our minds run back to the classic verse often printed on mugs and t-shirts: "'For I know the plans I have for you,' declares the LORD, 'plans to prosper you and not to harm you, plans to give you hope and a future'" (Jeremiah 29:11 NIV).

But when we only see that verse, we lose its context, and even a great balm for a hurting heart: "This is what the LORD says: "When seventy years are completed for Babylon, I will come to you and fulfill my good promise to bring you back to this place" (Jeremiah 29:10 NIV).

Do you see? God was saying, don't be scared. I've got this. It looks dark now, so I've given you my promise of a brighter future. Concentrate on my promise, not your heartache.

There are modern examples where heartache has purpose. Michael J. Fox wrote in his best-seller, *Lucky Man,* how the years of heartache became the best years of his life—not in spite of his illness, but because of it. Dealing with and coming to terms with his Parkinson's disease moved him from an ambitious, driven person to a more reflective and understanding one.

> "If you were to rush into this room right now and announce that you had struck a deal ... in which the ten years since my diagnosis could be magically taken away, traded in for ten more years as the person I was before—I would without a moment's hesitation tell you to take a hike .... I would never want to go back to that life—sheltered, narrow existence fueled by fear and made livable by insulation, isolation and self-indulgence."[24]

Consider television star Kathie Lee Gifford, who went through the heartbreak of public humiliation when she learned her husband, Frank Gifford, had an affair with a married flight attendant in 1997. "She thought her whole world was going to end," an insider exclusively told *Closer Weekly* .... "She told me she packed up her and the kids' bags at least twice, but she prayed her way through it."[25]

Coming to the realization that you typically will not die from a broken heart or from lost dreams doesn't come easy. These cries are clear. *Enough, God! I am over this. Do something already*! If your cries to God sound similar, take solace. You're in good company. Check out how noted prophet Habakkuk cried out to God in his heartache: "How long, O LORD, must I call for help? But you do not listen! 'Violence is everywhere!' I cry, but you do not come to save. Must I forever see these evil deeds? Why must I watch all this misery?" (Habakkuk 1:2-3 NLT).

The prophet Jeremiah (known as the weeping prophet) cried out as well, waiting for God to show up and rescue him: "Why then does my suffering continue? Why is my wound so incurable? Your help seems as uncertain as a seasonal brook, like a spring that has gone dry" (Jerimiah 15:18 NLT).

Like Habakkuk, I thought God didn't hear me. Or that my wounds felt incurable like Jeremiah's wounds.

I had to look deeper. I had to find out the truth about grace.

Is Grace Really Greater?

Kyle Idleman cuts to the chase in *Grace Is Greater*:

> "Is grace greater than even the pain caused by a drunk driver who kills your son? That's what the Bible says ... God's unconditional love is so transformative that the grace effect we experience will lead us to forgive even the worst of our worst enemies ... What the Bible is saying is that it is possible to get rid of our bitterness, rage, and

anger. The grace that flows to us through Jesus can flow from us to others. We can be set free from the prison of unforgiveness ... We can read Ephesians 4:32, 'Be kind and compassionate to one another, forgiving each other, just as in Christ God forgave you.'"[26]

It is possible to own that type of peace after heartache. But don't let me get ahead of myself. It doesn't come from hard work that *you* do.

Let's Look at You

We've looked at people in Scripture who dealt with heartache. We've read how contemporaries faced debilitating disease and devastation due to life-altering decisions made by someone else. What thread ties them all together? All those affected found the courage to leave heartache behind.

But what does that have to do with you?

It can be difficult to take in what I'm writing when your heart is so clearly broken into pieces. Your life has been toppled. But stay with me.

You've read that focusing on Truth and learning to trust that Truth is essential to getting through your calamity. How it's critical to trust that God has you in His hand and He is bigger than any problem you could place at his feet. Focus on this too:

Whatever heartache you feel, God feels it more.

He has dealt with heartache since sin entered the world. He had to banish man from the perfect Garden of Eden and watch mankind deal with the consequences of sin. Then, to give us a way back, He had to sacrifice His son for us before we ever knew Him. Before we loved Him back.

God understands pain. Yet He loves us beyond measure. The world that surrounds us tells us of God's lack of concern, yet

Christ is crying, "I am here for you!" Because of Jesus we can have confidence—yes, *confidence*—that whatever hurts our heart and upsets our life bothers God more. When we grieve, He feels it more. And when we hunger and reach out to him, He reaches back *even more*.

UNDER THE UMBRELLA

Write how focusing on Truth has either heightened or diminished your heartache?

_____

_____

_____

_____

_____

_____

_____

_____

_____

_____

_____

_____

_____

_____

_____

_____

Chapter Seven

Surrender

Journal entry: Thursday, April 7, 2011, 6:05 a.m.

Tick ... tick ... tick ... Time keeps slipping by; it is so precious. I embrace this opportunity to ponder my life. Has my faith been enough? It's helping to get me through yet another trying time, but it's never been tested before as it is now.
Is there enough grace for me ... for one more time?

The Morning's Prayer of Uncertainty

Father, I know what's happening, but I don't understand any of it. Why am I looking at the possibility of dying so soon? I know you love me, but, honestly, I don't get this brain tumor thing. Are you sure this is what you want for me?

G'morning, sweetheart. It's nice to see you in bed resting. Did you sleep well?"

Lew had no way of knowing I had been up most of the night writing emails. If I only had ten days to live, I wanted to tell as many people as possible that they had made a difference in my life and how I had been blessed by them. He didn't know that I had only crawled back into bed moments earlier.

"Well enough ... I think. It's Thursday. Do we have any plans?" I asked sarcastically, knowing we had a big day ahead of us.

"Not much goin' on," Lew said dryly. "Just need to see Dr. Powers, that's all. Think you could fit it in?"

I had spent hours digging through websites the day before, trying to understand brain tumors and what I could expect from the surgery. I read article after article on different techniques that Dr. Powers might use to remove my tumor. I watched a number of recorded procedures posted online.

My investigations offered certainties in my future: scalp-slicing and bone-cutting, with the goal of eradicating my tumor.

"Are you sure you want to see that stuff?" Lew asked when I told him what I had watched. "Doesn't it gross you out?"

"Not at all. I need to have complete faith in Dr. Powers. To do that, I need to understand what he's going to do. I'm sure he'll explain it to us in greater detail—as much detail as we want—but I need a point of reference when he does."

"We're seeing Dr. Powers in less than an hour. I'll make breakfast while you get dressed. Don't forget your list of questions."

I needed to be ready—ready to put myself in my surgeon's care. That meant being ready to surrender to his plan. To do that, I had to come from a place of trust and strength.

Surrendering to God

Surrendering to God is in no way a sign of weakness. It's a sign of trust. Proverbs reads, "The fear of the LORD is the beginning of wisdom, and knowledge of the Holy One is understanding" (Proverbs 9:10). Dwight L. Moody said it this way, "Let God have your life; He can do more with it than you can."[27]

But what does that mean? Simply stated, know where your responsibility ends and God's begins.

Lew and I didn't go into dealing with my brain tumor lightly. We also knew we were dealing with a crisis that reached beyond us. Because of our limitations. I'd spent hours searching the internet for information.

Talking with the medical team available to us was vital. We needed to share with them all the information they asked of us so they could make sound decisions. But we also knew without a doubt that God held me in the palm of His hand (Isaiah 49:16). My faith was being tested at every turn. And at each of those turns, God was with me.

I knew I needed to surrender to His plan.

Doing Your Part

Go back to the moment when your worst fell in on you. Remember some of your first thoughts? We covered them earlier: confusion and doubt. I suspect you also dealt with a huge portion of fear. Fear of what you knew as well as fear of the unknown. Often these responses have the power to freeze you in your tracks. The root of these feelings: Satan. Lying is a go-to move he often uses.[15] Scripture reminds us that "there is no truth in him [Satan]. When he lies, he speaks his native language, for he is a liar and the father of lies" (John 8:44 NIV).

How do you get past Satan's lies? Scripture.

In *Hope When It Hurts*,[28] Kristen Wetherell and Sarah Walton give examples of how to surrender to God after hearing the lies Satan has planted in your mind:

The Lie – Loneliness means I am alone.

The Truth – "Praise be to the God and Father of our Lord Jesus Christ, the Father of compassion and the God of all comfort, who comforts us in all

---

15   It's not that Satan and I are buddies, it's that I try to recognize his lies when I see them.

our troubles, so that we can comfort those in any trouble" (2 Corinthians 2:3-4 NIV).

The Lie – I am the only one who has suffered like this; no one understands my pain.

The Truth – Christ will not ask me to suffer anything He himself has not already suffered. If you doubt that, read Isaiah 53:3: "He was despised and rejected by mankind, a man of suffering, and familiar with pain. Like one from whom people hide their faces he was despised, and we held him in low esteem" (NIV).

Once you can differentiate between Satan's lies and God's truths, the process of surrendering your pain to God becomes more clear.

Processing Pain

It may be difficult to give up resentment and anger toward the focus of your pain.

If your pain stems from an incident with another person, this process will include communication. The goal is to work toward talking with the one who brought you such pain, explaining how the incident caused you harm. If you can't talk to the person directly, you may need to speak to professionals (lawyers or therapists for example) and use them as a conduit so they can help you process the tragedy. It can take days—even weeks or months—to complete this process. But in time, with dedication and healthy diligence and help, you can pass through this valley.

However, if your pain stems from a physical tragedy, where do you place your anger? Was it an accident? A drunk driver crossed the yellow line and changed your world forever. After the driver, who did you direct your anger toward? God?

You might think He should have prevented it.

How do you process the turmoil you're feeling with a God you resent? You treat Him like you'd treat the person who hurt you emotionally—through communication. Yell at God if that's what it takes to communicate. Afraid He'll get mad? He's a big God and can take your anger. Want to cry? Pull out a full box of tissues, and let out everything you have to cry about. You've just dealt with a life crisis. It deserves your tears. What God wants most from all of us is a relationship. Trusting Him with your anger is a great gift you can give to Him. It comes from a place of authenticity and honesty.

Sometimes yelling is a start. And crying. If yelling or crying doesn't help you dig deep into your soul and purge your anger, you may want to bring in professionals such as pastors or Christian therapists.[16]

You're not the first to be angry with God. Or, at the least, question Him. Check out Scripture:

Gideon asked an angel: "If the LORD is with us, why has all this happened to us?" (Judges 6:13 NIV).

Job says to God: "Though I cry, 'Violence!' I get no response; though I call for help, there is no justice" (Job 19:7 NIV).

The psalmist cried out to God: "Awake, Lord! Why do you sleep? Rouse yourself! Do not reject us forever" (Psalm 44:23 NIV).

Processing Anger with Honesty

Novelist Anne Lamont, who has written several books on loss, congratulates those who are honest enough with God to process their feelings, holding nothing back:

> "My belief is that when you're telling the truth, you're closer to God. If you say to God, 'I am exhausted and depressed beyond words, and I don't like you at all right now, and I recoil from

---

16   If you want to see a tongue-in-cheek look at this process, check out Angry Conversations with God: A Snarky but Authentic Spiritual Memoir by Susan E. Isaacs, where the author takes God to couples therapy.

most people who believe in You,' that might be the most honest thing you've ever said. If you told me you had to said to God, 'It's hopeless, and I don't have a clue if you exist, but I could use a hand,' it would almost bring tears to my eyes, tears of pride in you, for the courage it takes to get real—really real. It would make me want to sit next to you at the dinner table."[29]

Surrendering Makes You Whole

My heart began to open to God one morning after searching for His promises. I had to share it with Lew.

"Honey, Scripture tells us in Matthew 10:29-31 that a sparrow can't fall to the ground without it grieving God." I put my Bible down. "Huh. That's really something," I said. But my thoughts screamed *Could that be true for me?*

When dealing with a crisis, it's easy to feel as if God has taken His eyes off of you, turned His back for just a moment, or turned around, and said a holy *oopsie*. But that's another lie from Satan.

If you highlight lines in books to help you remember ... if you want to pull out a nugget to put on an index card and tape it to your bathroom mirror or clip it to your car's sun visor ... if you want a phrase to repeat before you go to bed, it is this:

> "Until we embrace the fact that only God is in control of our lives and not us, our faith will always falter. When we start to trust and surrender to God's plan—when we're ready to do a swan dive into the lap of Jesus and embrace what waits for us—our hearts will begin to heal. "

Hymnist Edward Mote (1797-1874) left out the swan dive analogy when he wrote "The Solid Rock," but he said it so well nonetheless:

"My hope is built on nothing less

82

Than Jesus' blood and righteousness;
I dare not trust the sweetest frame,
But wholly lean on Jesus' name.
On Christ, the solid Rock, I stand;
All other ground is sinking sand."

Time Test Challenge

Know that Satan works double time when we're on the ropes. Depression most likely creeps in to keep you in bed—all day every day. If that's where you are right now, I am not judging you. I *understand* you. But I challenge you to do a Time Test with God. It's pretty easy, even when dealing with thoughts too dark to mention. It consists of a prayer and a bit of action on your part. The prayer goes something like this:

Father, Your Word tells me you will never leave me nor forsake me, but I feel very alone. (Name the issue of your fear. Are you angry? Fearful? Suicidal? Be honest. God knows, but He needs you to express exactly what you're feeling and why you're feeling it.)

Father, I'm going to set a timer for fifteen minutes and trust that You will keep me safe for that period of time. I surrender everything to You right now and trust You are in control. Amen.

When the buzzer sounds and the fifteen minutes are over, smile ... you made it! Now, set the timer again. Do it for another fifteen minutes. Here's your next prayer:

Father, I've set a timer for fifteen minutes again. You blessed me with life through the previous block of time, please help me with the next block. I can't do this without You. I surrender my pain and situation to You. Thank You for staying close. Amen.

Do this again and again—do it all day. Change your fifteen minutes to thirty. You can do this. God will meet you. He will prove to be faithful. He loves brokenhearted people—and right now, dear one, that is you.

Surrendering seldom feels comfortable. It goes against how we try to take care of ourselves. But to trust God is to surrender to Him. And it has to come from a place of vigorous honesty. Don't think that it's a one-and-done event. The secret is a willingness to ask God to meet you where you are—to meet you in your worst. Maybe even at your worst.

He'll be there. He's waiting for your invitation.

UNDER THE UMBRELLA

How can you trust and surrender to God for good things when you cannot see or feel him?

_____

_____

_____

_____

_____

_____

_____

_____

_____

_____

_____

_____

_____

_____

_____

_____

_____

_____

Chapter Eight

Faith

Journal entry: Friday, April 8, 2011, 2:51 p.m.

This is what I know ...
In three days I'm having brain surgery. My Monday morning schedule is:

- *I have to be at the hospital @ 7:30*
- *I have one last MRI scheduled for 9:30 before surgery*
- *Surgery is scheduled to begin @ 10:45*
- *This is slated to be a six-hour surgery, so I don't imagine information on my condition will be available until after 5:00*
- *If all goes well, they plan to have me stay in the ICU for 24-48 hours with only limited visitors.*

That is ... if all goes well.

The Morning's Prayer of Uncertainty

Father, thank You for the glimpse You've given me into Your plan for my life. I don't know why I have this tumor in my head. I don't know how this ordeal will end. All I know is that right now—at this very moment—my faith in You is unwavering. Your presence is tangible. Does this mean You'll soon be escorting me home? Is that why You're so real to me? It's Your call, Lord. Your will be done. As long as I still have You close.

W hy Lord? Can't You see I'm stretched to my limit?
That's a mouthful.

"Now faith is confidence in what we hope for and assurance about what we do not see" (Hebrews 11:1 NIV).

Another mouthful.

Because you're reading this book, my guess is you've come face-to-face with a circumstance that has rocked your world. Not only have your knees buckled from the emotional weight, but most things around you indicate God isn't a good god like you had thought. At this very moment, whether you're cognizant of it or not, a question may be looming in your mind: *Who is God and why is His love being expressed with tragedy?*

Here's the frustrating truth: God is who He is, because that's who He says He is.

I appreciate Lydia Brownback's perception on this conundrum:

"God often acts contrary to how we think a good god should act. The answer we think we need seems so logical and clear to our way of thinking, yet God does not provide it. That is where faith comes in. Real faith isn't the belief that God will do a particular thing; real faith is the conviction that God is good, no matter what he does and however he chooses to answer our prayers. God always has our best in mind and he works to bring it about, no matter how it may look initially to our way of thinking."[30]

The Process of Regaining Faith

Circumstances that confound us need not drive us to despair. Instead, they can take us to new depths. The process to regain faith is simple—but don't for a moment think it's easy. As we saw in the last chapter, surrendering to God's plan is vital. After your heart surrenders, it can accept the fact that God has a plan—a *good* plan. Charles Stanley's article *Rebuilding Your Faith*[31] visits three steps for having a closer relationship with God:

☑ *Make a decision to choose to believe that God is trustworthy and faithful.* God always keeps His promises. He desires the best for our lives. At times, what we think is the best and what He knows is the best may be conflicting. However, God's ways always produce the most spiritual fruit, the strongest character, and the unimaginable perfect result.

☑ *Refuse to doubt God.* The enemy hopes to thwart us by infusing doubt into our minds that will lead us to question our faith. When we refuse to look at our circumstances through worldly eyes, God gives us a sense of peace and rest.

☑ *Read God's Word and meditate on His promises.* Searching the Bible for God's promises is one way we can quiet the wavering of our faith, standing on all His promises with the deep assurance that God always keeps His Word.

Remember God's promise: "Never will I leave you. Never will I forsake you" (Hebrews 13:5 NIV). During this period of darkness, if you haven't surrendered your heart to God, that promise may seem empty. But a surrendered heart will hold on to those words like a lifeline. Trust that comfort and strength will be found there.

Having and Being Enough

As Craig Groeschel explained in *Hope in the Dark,* "Habakkak grew into a person with a richer faith, a faith that may not have developed as fully had he not struggled through his doubts."[32]

That was my story as well. If I had understood why I had the brain tumor and that good would come from it, I wouldn't have needed faith. It would have been about me and what I could do to control the situation. But from the time I heard God whisper *Do you trust me?* I could feel His love. Sense His presence. I knew it in my *Knower.*[17]

Lew and I knew my tumor was no accident. We knew God had a purpose for what was happening. We hungered for sound medical support and prayer. There were no contingency plans. We trusted that the medical team and our faith in *Jehovah Rapha* would be enough. We knew His plan for my life had started earlier—even before time began.[33] And we knew He would see it through to fruition—whatever that meant.

There are several stories in Scripture about people who knew what they knew as well. We meet Elisha in 1 Kings 19 when God sent Elijah to find his successor. Elisha seemed to have a peaceful, untroubled life when Elijah found him plowing his field. When Elijah "threw his cloak around Elisha," (v 19), Elisha only slowed to kiss his parents and tell them goodbye. He then burned the plow he was using and slaughtered the oxen, giving it to the people for food (v.20). He left his family and livelihood to follow God. There was no turning back for Elisha. He was all in.

The New Testament is also filled with people of great faith. Consider the Apostle Paul, the author of more than half of the New Testament. His passion for the Lord was obvious—Jesus was the focal point of all his thoughts. In 2 Corinthians 11:24-31 he shares with great candor and without filter of what was done to him to shake his faith:

---

17   As a reminder from Chapter 5, your Knower is that place in your being where there are no doubts. Where you carry truth that sometimes has no explanation. Still, you know it's true. Your Knower tells you so.

"Five times I received from the Jews the forty lashes minus one. Three times I was beaten with rods, once I was pelted with stones, three times I was shipwrecked, I spent a night and a day in the open sea, I have been constantly on the move. I have been in danger from rivers, in danger from bandits, in danger from my fellow Jews, in danger from Gentiles; in danger in the city, in danger in the country, in danger at sea; and in danger from false believers. I have labored and toiled and have often gone without sleep; I have known hunger and thirst and have often gone without food; I have been cold and naked. Besides everything else, I face daily the pressure of my concern for all the churches. Who is weak, and I do not feel weak? Who is led into sin, and I do not inwardly burn? If I must boast, I will boast of the things that show my weakness. The God and Father of the Lord Jesus, who is to be praised forever, knows that I am not lying."

Be Ever Vigilant

Biblical authors did not stand around scratching their heads and asking, "Why do bad things happen to good people?" They knew Satan's *modus operandi* and that this world is a spoiled planet ruled by the father of lies. What else should they expect but ugliness?

Satan is always watching for chinks in our faith. While you work diligently to focus your faith, Satan is just as busy trying to steal your aim.[34] While you're dealing with intense heartache, he may bring past regrets to mind, challenge you to blame innocent people for the pain you're swimming in, or tell you that your God doesn't care.

During my ten days of waiting, God stayed closer to me than He ever had, and He began restoring my faith. I read powerful passages, "If you look for me wholeheartedly, you will find me" (Jeremiah 29:13 NLT) and claimed the promises for my own. I also read passages that touched hidden areas of my heart: "I will repay you for the years the locusts have eaten—the great locust and the young locust, the other locusts and the locust swarm—my great army that I sent among you. You will have plenty to eat, until you are full, and you will praise the name of the LORD YOUR GOD, who has worked wonders for you; never again will my people be shamed" (Joel 2:25-26 NIV).

God is on your side. He wants you to have victory over this crisis. But it may take work.

The Power of Choice

What does choosing faith in God have to do with getting through a catastrophe?

Faith matures when, after being pressed down from trials, it still endures. Know this:

A faith that is tested by fire is a faith that can be trusted.

You can read all the stories in the Bible you want, but it isn't until your faith has been through the fire and God has sustained that you will you be able to trust He'll be there again.

We all have a choice in how we view tragedy. It'd be crazy to celebrate someone betraying a trust, an unfavorable diagnosis, or the tragedy of the death of a dear friend. We need to deal with our feelings. However, when we choose to downplay the situation— retreat from our pain or soft-pedal our devastation—we're not trusting God. We're still trying to control our surroundings. If we don't trust His plan, we may miss the opportunity for growth and great blessings that He has waiting for us.

When standing on faith in God, life's situations—no matter how dire—take on a new perspective. Recalling Mother Theresa and her years living with those in India's abject poverty, her situation never changed. Babies died. Children starved. Women found no justice. But she reached millions with her unshakable faith in the God she served.

We, too, can ask God to help build our faith with prayers that reach beyond our comprehension. When tragedy hits, it takes tremendous faith to accept that God has good waiting for us. Hear His words of love as shared by Isaiah, "See, I am doing a new thing! Now it springs up; do you not perceive it? I am making a way in the wilderness and streams in the wasteland" (Isaiah 43:19).

God is not intimidated or put off by huge prayers. Steven Furtick's *Sun Stand Still: What Happens When You Dare to Ask God for The Impossible*[35] is filled with story after story of audacious prayers.

When I re-evaluated my faith in God, I retreated to a quiet place and pushed into my diagnosis, then on to painful memories, feeling every disappointment that surrounded them. If I was to count on God to help me get through the next few days, I couldn't retreat or refuse this process.

After long hours of self-examination, I realized if I was truly going to ask Him to heal my heart, I needed to bring light to my past bad choices, confess any hidden sin, and then stand firm on my faith, knowing that my Lord's word would stand true.[36] I repented every bad choice that came to mind. I reflected on all the necessary consequences I had faced and pondered the outcome of them all. Finally, with a clean heart, I could ask for His help.

This Can't Be Happening

Dealing with devastation has the capability of shaking a faith to its very foundation. All our lofty principles and spiritual views are clouded when seen through the fragmented lens of a devastated situation. Often, an early response is anger. Unfortunately, many lessons we learned from Sunday school tell us it's "unchristian" to react in that manner.

Really?

Stand back and objectively look at what you're in the middle of right now. Don't you think anger fits? Our challenge is to not sin in our anger (Ephesians 4:26). That's the rub.

You've just had your world fall apart. Maybe you've been told you can't have children. Or maybe the stock market tanked and took most of your savings. At times like this, the last thing we may want is to upset God by bringing our true ugly self to His feet. Instead, we become less authentic. We stuff our feelings and do our best to be a good soldier and somehow pull through.

But just pulling through denies our relationship with Christ to flourish. If there is ever a time to pull close to Jesus, it's during a tragedy. But if there are unspoken resentments or anger, don't you see how that would affect your faith?

Setting Vigil

Read the account of a father dealing with his possessed son in Mark 9:21-24 (NIV):

> "Jesus asked the boy's father, 'How long has he been like this?'
>
> 'From childhood,' he answered. 'It has often thrown him into fire or water to kill him. But if you can do anything, take pity on us and help us.'
>
> 'If you can?' said Jesus. 'everything is possible for one who believes.'
>
> Immediately the boy's father exclaimed, 'I do believe; help me overcome my disbelief.'"

Paraphrased into today's language, the verse would read something like this: "Oh, Lord, I want to believe. Father in Heaven, I do. But I don't. I'm struggling. Really struggling. Help me overcome my disbelief and doubts."

Building faith takes tenacity. The battle is real. What are you fighting against? Do you feel as if others have taken advantage of you? Has the situation you're in left you completely numb, with no feelings at all? Do what you can to reach past your pain. God is waiting, but you have to participate. Are you willing to ask honest questions? To wrestle? And, more importantly, are you willing to listen to what God has to say?

God's Healing Presence

Is there a reconciliation story that needs to unfold in *your* life? Is there an enemy you need to forgive, to do good to or to be reconciled with? Who is it? Your best friend? An abusive spouse? Your church leaders? A drunk driver? What do you need to do?

You can do this. Grace is greater than your hurt. Finding that grace takes faith.

Let God's grace—and your faith in God—flow.

UNDER THE UMBRELLA

Moment of truth: Is your heart open to having faith in God? Through complete transparency, write your reservations about trusting God and what it would take to rid yourself of them.

_____

_____

_____

_____

_____

_____

_____

_____

_____

_____

_____

_____

_____

_____

_____

_____

Chapter Nine

Gratitude

Journal entry: Saturday, April 9, 2011, 5:38 a.m.

It's been a week now—just seven days ago I had the seizure and heard the word tumor—and my life has been changed forever.

The Morning's Prayer of Uncertainty

Life is falling into place, Father, but I need to feel close to You today. I need to see Your presence surrounding me as I deal with what's at hand. Is this really what You want? Does this really have to happen?

*R*obs," Lew yelled from the back of the house, "Do you hear that? Sounds like someone's at the door. Can you get it?"

Saturday's plans were to rest after all of the errands and preparations Lew and I had accomplished. I looked forward to hanging around the house, writing more notes, and connecting with people I needed to reach. My time was limited, and I had so much to do—so much to say.

I looked out the door's window as I walked up and saw, Grant, a friend from church, standing there smiling with a towel wrapped around something oblong and flat.

"Hope I'm not disturbing you," he said, "but Kate made a casserole for you guys. I know you won't be cooking for a while, and if your kids come to stay you'll need some extra food." After we shared a few pleasantries, he went his way with a wave and a hearty, "God bless you guys."

I took the covered dish to the kitchen, then settled down to write more notes. The cool morning welcomed the afternoon sunlight as it washed the room.

Once I settled into my coveted spot, the phone rang. Tami, another friend from church, was on the line. After a bit of small talk, she got down to the purpose of her call.

"Robin, I imagine you'll be out of commission after surgery. How about we set a time for me to come over and clean your house? I know Lew's going to do his best, but if you'd like a woman's touch to cap it off, I'd love to help out."

"Tami, that's perfect. Thank you." I knew Lew's plans included housekeeping, but he and I both knew his sense of what it took to clean differed from mine. Tami's offer of help made me feel more confident in the outcome.

After Tami's call, I went back to my correspondence. However, the lack of sleep and constant emotional drain were beginning to affect me. As I leaned back to rest my eyes, another set of knocks rapped on the door.

Fran, Lew's supervisor stood outside. We greeted him together and joined him on the front porch.

"Hi Robin. Lew." Fran shuffled his feet. "You guys look great. I can't stay long." Still shuffling.

"Thanks, Fran," Lew started, "for working out a plan where I can work from home for the next few months." I had only met Fran a couple of times and was pleasantly surprised to see him.

"No problem. Take all the time you need." Fran stood on the porch, shifting his weight from one foot to another. He reached into his pocket. "Some of us at the office got a gift certificate to a home delivery food service. You tell them what you want, and they bring it right to you. We wanted to let you guys know we're thinking about you."

"Thanks, Fran," Lew said, taking the gift card. "And thank the crew back at the office."

Fran continued to shift from one foot to another. When I had the opportunity to speak with him before this, he came across as the type of guy who never got emotional. I saw my assessment was pretty spot on. Apparently, dealing with touchy-feely circumstances was not his strong suit. "Yea, sure, you bet. Can't stay too long, you guys. Let us know if you need anything." With those few words, Fran left.

Again, I settled into writing emails to folks I wanted to connect with. A few minutes passed, and I heard another knock at the door.

"For the love of—"

I looked out the door window, but didn't see anyone there.

Knock, knock, knock.

With the second set of knocks, I opened the door to see Sophie, our two-year-old neighbor, with a poster-sized picture in her hands. Just then, her daddy walked up. Sophie's parents had seen the EMTs put me in the ambulance and had tried to keep in touch with us during the week.

"Sophie thought you may need a picture for your room while you rest," he said. Sophie's face beamed with delight as she offered me the finger-painted masterpiece. In a tiny voice, she described each scribble and streak of color.

"I will hang it proudly," I said. "In fact, I'll put it up where it will be the first thing I see when I awake." Sophie smiled, folded her cute little arms across her chest, and strode off.

After I closed the door, the revelation of what had been happening over the past few hours hit me. I turned to Lew, "God really is everywhere—so many people reaching out to support us, even little Sophie. I needed God to be big for me today."

I needed assurance that He loved me with a complete, perfect love. And He came through—in knocks at the door and gift cards and pictures drawn by a two-year-old.

Learning Gratitude

Complaining about our status—our plight—causes us to focus on our less-than-perfect situation. Gratitude, on the other hand, isn't void of the circumstances, but focuses on God's grace in its midst. And God's grace is reason enough to be grateful.

Choosing gratitude takes practice.

Phil Hansen[37] rocked the art world with his style of pointillism, until he began experiencing a tremor in his hand. This was pure devastation for the artist. Instead of commiserating with Phil over his loss, his neurologist challenged him to *embrace the shake*. Phil explains, "It's not easy to 'embrace the shake.' We have grown up learning we need to highlight our strengths and hide our weaknesses. We don't embrace our limitations; we're embarrassed by them, so much so we often refuse to admit them. We need to first be limited in order to become limitless."[38]

Because Phil accepted that he had to let go of his dream of being the type of artist he had studied to be and begin to embrace who he was now, his weakness became his strength. Not only has he changed his art style from pointillism to creativity art, he's become an internationally-sought inspirational speaker on how we can strive to work within our limitations.

Apostle Paul said, "Give thanks in all circumstances; for this is God's will for you in Christ Jesus" (1 Thessalonians 5:18 NIV). It doesn't say *for* everything, but *in* everything.

Life can be harsh. God gives us grace and never asks us to deny our reality. That includes a life that is difficult, cruel, sad, or even tragic. What we have is the love of a heavenly Father who is always there waiting for us.

But it's still a bitter pill to swallow.

Once again, here we rely on what we know and what we feel. We never know when our feelings of gratitude will catch up with a life that suits our hearts. It's a lesson we may need to learn—and relearn—every day. But when gratitude becomes a part of your life's routine, it will pay back in sweet dividends.

The Gift That Keeps on Giving

Research from *Harvard Health Publications* offers that the more we complain, the more we have to complain about.[39] In this study, two groups were formed. The first was told to keep an "irritation journal" and the second to keep a "thanksgiving journal." The researchers discovered that those with the thanksgiving journals had more energy and enthusiasm, slept better, and were less depressed. Those with the irritation journals became increasingly discontented.

Try it out in your life. Start slowly. Realize you have more to be thankful for than not.

Can't see it? Let me help you.

Put your hand on your chest. Feel your heart beating? Feel your chest rise and fall as air enters your lungs? That's life. You did nothing to earn it. Nothing about you made it begin. It's a gift to you. That's something to be thankful for. Now move on to other reasons for gratitude. Your clothes. Your next meal. The roof over your head. All to be thankful for.

When you continue this exercise, you'll be surprised at how seeing life through the eyes of gratitude warms the coldest of hearts. Circumstances may not change. Your tragedy may be just as targeted at you as before. But when you look at your life through a wider lens, all the pieces come into focus.

God's Thoughts on Complaining

God takes complaining personally, because it overlooks the greatness of the grace He offers. Complaining short-changes the promises of the gospel and passes right over God's mercy. Can you see why God finds complaining offensive? At its crux, complaining says "I don't believe God is loving after all. He doesn't care for me like Scripture says." Bottom line, complaining rejects God and His grace for your life.

Jesus had loads of opportunities to complain. But He knew there was a purpose for His time on earth. God the Father had sent God the Son to rescue us—each of us—from the sin that ripples through each of our lives. He knew what the cost of covering our sins was. Jesus not only knew He was following the will of the Father, He knew by paying for *our* sins we had the chance to live forever in paradise. Imagine Jesus' gratitude when He cried, "It is finished" (John 19:30). Not only was His physical pain over from being a man, He had accomplished what He had been sent to do.

Guard Your Heart

When Joni Eareckson Tada suffered a diving accident at the age of sixteen that left her a quadriplegic, she begged God to take her life. She even begged her friends to help her end her torment. But she became a popular Christian writer, artist, and motivational speaker. Sounds pretty sweet, right?

Don't forget, she is a quadriplegic.

She tells a story to remind us of gratitude:

> "Honesty is always the best policy, but especially when you're surrounded by a crowd of women in a restroom during a break at a Christian women's conference. One woman, putting on her lipstick, said, 'Oh, Joni, you always look so together, so happy in your wheelchair. I wish I had your joy!' Several women nodded. 'How do you do it?' she asked as she capped her lipstick.
>
> 'I don't do it,' I said. 'In fact, may I tell you honestly how I woke up this morning?'
>
> 'This is an average day.' I breathed in deeply. 'After

my husband, Ken, leaves for work at 6:00 a.m., I'm alone until I hear the front door open at 7:00 a.m. That's when a friend arrives to get me up. While I listen to her make coffee, I pray, *Oh Lord, my friend will soon give me a bath, get me dressed, sit me up in my chair, brush my hair and teeth, and send me out the door. I don't have the strength to face this routine one more time. I have no resources. I don't have a smile to take into the day. But you do. May I have yours? God, I need you desperately.*

'So, what happens when your friend comes through the bedroom door?' one of them asked.

'I turn my head toward her and give her a smile sent straight from heaven. It's not mine. It's God's. And so,' I gesture to my paralyzed legs, 'whatever joy you see today was hard won this morning.'

I have learned that the weaker we are, the more we need to lean on God; and the more we lean on God, the stronger we discover him to be."[40]

Joni learned soon after her accident to protect her heart and mind. She prayed throughout the day and spoke words of affirmation to herself. Complaining over her circumstances—and her circumstances were dire—would not help her. It would only cause her more pain.

It's not easy processing a tragedy with gratitude, but what choices are there? Remember this wisdom from Peter, "Be alert and of sober mind. Your enemy the devil prowls around like a roaring lion looking for someone to devour" (1 Peter 5:8).

One of the ways Satan tries to devour us is through the lack of gratitude.

Apostle Paul also had reason to complain. Everywhere he traveled, it was always the same: find the local synagogue, speak on the love, death, and resurrection of Jesus, get beat up and kicked out of the city or jailed, only to do it all over again. How did God bless Paul? By giving him a "thorn in his side."

> "I was given a thorn in my flesh, a messenger of Satan, to torment me. Three times I pleaded with the Lord to take it away from me. But he said to me, 'My grace is sufficient for you, for my power is made perfect in weakness.' Therefore I will boast all the more gladly about my weaknesses, so that Christ's power may rest on me. That is why, for Christ's sake, I delight in weaknesses, in insults, in hardships, in persecutions, in difficulties. For when I am weak, then I am strong?" (2 Corinthians 12: 7-12 NIV).

When you're at your lowest is when Satan speaks the loudest. *Does God really love you? Forget Him. He's not even real.* Have you heard similar thoughts? Don't think for a moment that these are random ideas. Read and ponder the many words of Apostle Peter and Apostle Paul through the New Testament. There you will read of great suffering, only to be matched with greater gratitude.

Let me put you on notice: Satan is attacking you through your thoughts. But you can rise above all the pain he has in store for you. You can combat him—and win—with prayer and gratitude.

UNDER THE UMBRELLA

It may be difficult, but make a gratitude list.

_____

_____

_____

_____

_____

_____

_____

_____

_____

_____

_____

_____

_____

_____

_____

_____

_____

_____

Chapter Ten

Peace

Journal entry: Sunday, April 10, 2011, 3:53 a.m.

Another early morning and I'm wide awake, alone with my thoughts. These last few days have been the longest days of my life. Not only has this tragedy seemed to slow down time, it has also pulled life into focus.
God, help me be strong, if only once more.

The Morning's Prayer of Uncertainty

This is my last day before surgery, Father. I've heard of miraculous healings. Do You have one waiting for me?

Sunday. The day before surgery, and my heart was filled with needs. I needed to be in church and worship with my church family. I needed to press through one last time and hug people's necks—many of whom have made a difference in my life. And I needed to hear the sermon and the words God meant especially for me.

Lew and I filled the morning with normal activity. We got ready for church, but a sense of foreboding hung in the air. We wanted normalcy, but this day couldn't be any farther from it. Throughout the morning, when our fingers happened to touch, they lingered a bit longer than usual. Laughter that had once come easily between us was now washed with preoccupation.

Lew exaggerated a bounce to his step, seeming to offer his best effort to keep my spirits up. I'd watched as he waited for the other shoe to drop—for me to melt into a puddle of tears—but my resilience had stayed strong. Even though there had been moments I'd fought to hold back tears over the past nine days, our lives thus far had been tear free. While I was terrified, I was basking in a sense of real peace.

"Today," I said, getting out of the car at church, "I want to take everything that's offered. I want to accept hugs and well wishes as they come. And God has something for me today. I just know He does."

When the worship music began to fill the auditorium, tears washed my eyes. Standing with my church family, singing praises to God as one voice, humbled my heart. My soul felt like it would burst from gratitude.

Thank You, Father. Thank You for this group of people.

Standing next to Lew, I calmly knelt in my place. With outstretched arms, I sang along with *Here I Am to Worship* and opened myself the best I could to experience God's presence. I had never knelt in my pew before, and it didn't matter that my actions were different than that of those around me. People may have thought I acted fanatically, but I needed to get through to God, and I wasn't going to apologize for being so demonstrative.

God is in This

Christianity has gotten a bad rap because well-meaning Christians try to pretend they have everything figured out. Even down to how to manufacture peace. But when you're dealing with parents whose son was killed in a military skirmish or a woman who's just learned her cancer came back, you need more than manufactured peace.

You need the real deal.

As you've read this book you've worked hard to find God's best in your worst. You've battled with confusion, doubt, and heartache. You've learned that preparation is necessary in difficult times to establish (or re-establish) trust, faith, and gratitude. You've surrendered to the process. And I congratulate you. All this is for your peace.

Your worst may have happened years ago, and you've just begun the healing process. You're tired of white-knuckling[18] your way through the pain. It's my hope that you see God has been with you in the middle of your pain, waiting for you to reach out to Him. You can still choose to trust God. It's never too late.

No matter what or when tragedy happened, how painfully your heart was pierced, or how devastating the news was that you received, you can continue to take one more step into one more day. In peace.

As with Habakkuk, your prayers become more honest about what you've lost or will lose when you realize you still have God. You can say with unwavering confidence, "Even though I don't like it, even though I don't understand it, even though I know He could and He should but He's not, yet will I trust in the Lord my God."[41]

God Can Bring Good from Unpleasantness

There are few things in this world we can control, but one thing we can manage is how we respond to life around us. Our choice is simple: we can either dissolve under pressure or we can praise God in the midst of any situation and rise to the occasion.[42] Choosing to respond to my brain tumor and possible ten-day death sentence by turning to God caused my faith to grow exponentially.

---

18   It's like a rollercoaster ride or holding the hand of a woman in labor. Pretty intense.

One of my favorite examples of accepting our circumstances and God's will comes from Corrie ten Boom's story of being in the Ravensbrück concentration camp.[43] There, Corrie, her sister Betsie, and hundreds of other women lived in flea-plagued barracks. In all the other barracks, the Nazi guards walked through them at their pleasure. Leaving the women no room for privacy. But because of the flea infestation in their living quarters, the guards would not enter. Corrie and the other women huddled under a dim and bare lightbulb that hung in the back, away from where the guards could see when they looked in the opened door. Away from where they could see them reading Scripture from a smuggled Bible.

Despite the extreme unpleasantness of their circumstances, these women read the Bible in Dutch and translations were passed on in German, French, Polish, Russian, and Czech. Though their skin festered with bug bites, the hearts of these women from different countries, stolen from their homes, could find comfort from God's presence.

Corrie, influenced by the wisdom of her sister, Betsie, chose to seek God's plan in her hideous situation. Because she chose to embrace God's blessings—however slight they seemed—spiritual peace permeated the barracks and God's Word spread.

Because of Betsie's heart for God. Because of fleas.

She and the other women in the barracks controlled their attitudes.

Allow God to Show You His Glory

Maybe your turnaround moment doesn't come. The cancer spreads. The wayward spouse doesn't return. Sometimes no amount of praying, fasting, or righteous living seems to help. Tragedy still comes. But God can reveal His glory anyway.

After Sunday lunch at our favorite eatery, Lew and I headed home. I looked forward to throwing on a pair of sweats and relaxing. However, once I had changed, the phone rang. Lew picked it up, chatted for a moment, then muted the phone and walked over to me as I nestled on the couch.

"You may want to take this."

"Who is it?"

"She told me her name, but I don't know her." Looking puzzled, he continued. "She lives in Oregon. Do we know anyone who lives in Oregon?"

"Well," I said pushing back the afghan, "we do now."

"Hello, this is Robin," I said into the receiver. "Who is this?"

"Hi, Robin," a voice said on the other end of the line. "My name is Janice. You don't know me, but I read your blog, then went to your CaringBridge[19] site, and I wanted to reach out to you. I've had brain tumors and survived the surgery that removed them. I thought maybe we could chat. I'd love to offer any insight to you regarding what's happening right now and maybe what you can expect to deal with afterward."

Janice and I talked for almost an hour. We talked about brain tumors and neurosurgeons, our fears, our families, and how inadequacies try to overtake us. We talked about our children and how they were affected. We talked about a number of unknowns she had dealt with and the unknowns waiting for me. With questions asked and fears in the open, she turned the conversation.

"Dark is dark and fear is fear; it's all real," Janice said. "But I know someone who is larger than all that. His name is Jesus."

"*I know Jesus too*. And he's offering a peace I've never experience before!"

Janice and I shared a bit of our stories—how we each came to know Christ and how our lives had been enriched because of our experiences—both good and bad ones.

"You know God is working through your ordeal, don't you?" Janice asked. "You know His plans are perfect, right?"

"Yes, I do, but, Janice, I'm still scared. How is that?"

"It's normal to be afraid, because you're human. I'm glad to hear you're not focusing on your tumor or surgery. They are what

---

19   Caringbridge.org is a free website and app for families dealing with difficult medical times. It allows notes, photos, and updates to be passed on those interested in the health and well-being of a friend or family member.

they are. Your focus needs to be elsewhere. It's good you know that. Can I pray with you before I hang up?"

I welcomed her sensitivity as she began praying. She prayed for my physical, emotional, and spiritual health. She thanked me for taking the time to chat.

Then she was gone.

Having a woman from the other side of the country who I'd never met before call me the day before my surgery and comfort me as only she could is an example of God showing His glory.

Becoming Real

God is just as real during a storm as He is during tranquility. Know—without a doubt—that God has not abandoned you in this moment of need. Remember how Habakkuk concludes his prayer, "The Sovereign LORD is my strength; he makes my feet like the feet of a deer, he enables me to tread on the heights" (Habakkuk 3:19 NIV). His plan is real and His purpose for you is steadfast. In that, you can find peace.

Take this to heart. God loves you with an unwavering love, and His plan has always been the same—for you to accomplish His purpose. Perhaps you veered off the path of good choices a bit, but let me repeat, *God's plan has always been steadfast.* Read Psalm 139, and rest in its peace:

> "God, investigate my life; get all the facts firsthand. I'm an open book to you; even from a distance, you know what I'm thinking. You know when I leave and when I get back; I'm never out of your sight. You know everything I'm going to say before I start the first sentence. I look behind me and you're there, then up ahead and you're there, too—your reassuring presence, coming and going. This is too much, too wonderful—I can't take it all in!
>
> Is there anyplace I can go to avoid your Spirit? To

be out of your sight? If I climb to the sky, you're there! If I go underground, you're there! If I flew on morning's wings to the far western horizon, you'd find me in a minute—you're already there waiting! Then I said to myself, 'Oh, he even sees me in the dark! At night I'm immersed in the light!' It's a fact: darkness isn't dark to you; night and day, darkness and light, they're all the same to you.

Oh yes, you shaped me first inside, then out; you formed me in my mother's womb. I thank you, High God—you're breathtaking! Body and soul, I am marvelously made! I worship in adoration— what a creation! You know me inside and out, you know every bone in my body; you know exactly how I was made, bit by bit, how I was sculpted from nothing into something. Like an open book, you watched me grow from conception to birth; all the stages of my life were spread out before you, the days of my life all prepared before I'd even lived one day" (Psalm 139:1-16 THE MESSAGE).

Peace rests in Scripture. Embrace it. It's waiting for you. Don't allow suffering to steal the peace of God.

Suffering has the potential to embitter a spirit, harden a heart, and paralyze a will. Choosing suffering over peace keeps us from the opportunities God has in store for us. It requires all of our attention and drains us of God's positive resources, leaving us feeling like we have nothing left to give.

It's your choice. You've worked so hard up to this point, and it's all been to gain peace. Don't stop now.

UNDER THE UMBRELLA

We are often our own worst enemy when it comes to our healing and spiritual growth. As you face uncertainty, what does it take for you to accept God's unwavering peace?

_____

_____

_____

_____

_____

_____

_____

_____

_____

_____

_____

_____

_____

_____

_____

_____

Chapter Eleven

Grace

Journal entry: Monday, April 11, 2011, 1:00 a.m.

I can only imagine how difficult the next passing hours will be for Lew, my children and friends and family. I hope they know I am confident that everything will go as it has been designed—whatever that means.

I need to focus on my "journey of purpose" and "He who began a good work in Robin Luftig will carry it on to completion until the day of Christ Jesus" (Philippians 1:6) (So, okay, I took a few liberties with Scripture, but I needed to make it personal).

I woke up extra early on Monday, April 11, 2011. It had always been Lew's custom to bring coffee to bed for us each morning. Having breakfast and welcoming the sun as it rose over the Susquehanna River was a daily ritual. Today, however, I wanted to serve Lew.

"You only bring the coffee on weekends," he said, surprised as I walked in with a cup for him. "Today is Monday."

"I know, and don't worry. I'm not drinking before surgery. Today's coffee is only for you." I paused. "I don't know if or when I'll be able to bring you coffee in bed again." Another pause. "Hopefully I can do this again soon."

Grace.

I looked for it. I hoped the outcome would be as I wanted. But I had no guarantees. But it is in our human blindness that God's grace works. There is always enough. No matter how many tears we offer Him, and no matter how big our void from pain, His grace can meet our need.

Every. Time.

And you're never in a better situation to encounter and embrace that grace than the moment you understand you don't have what it takes—that God's grace is all you need. Read again Apostle Paul's view on his need for grace.

> "But he [God] said to me, 'My grace is sufficient
> for you, for my power is made perfect in weakness.'
> Therefore I will boast all the more gladly about my
> weaknesses, so that Christ's power may rest on me"
> (2 Corinthians 12:9 NIV).

In *Grace is Greater,* Kyle Idleman cautions the reader that grace can sometimes be hard:

> "I know when you're going through suffering or
> you're living with pain, it may seem that God,
> who is all-powerful, should do something to help.
> Consider the possibility that God in his grace is
> helping. Sometimes grace hurts so that it can
> help. It's hard to find grace in cancer, but maybe
> God allows the cancer to help us take stock of our
> lives and help us and those around us think about

eternity. It's hard to find God's grace when you can't stand your boss, but maybe God allows a difficult boss to help us learn to be self-controlled and not find identity in our job.

He is at work within us to make us more like Jesus. It may not make any sense now, but just keep reading.

In some cases, we'll have to keep reading all the way into eternity, the tension between 'Life is Hard' and 'God is good' won't be fully reconciled until we are with him in heaven. But from the perspective of heaven we will finally be able to see the greatness of God's grace. Paul talks about this in 2 Corinthians 4:17-18: God will bring good out of your bad. And even if you can't currently see how God might be drawing you closer or getting glory from your pain, you still need to remember, you're in the middle. This isn't the end of your story. Just keep reading. Grace will have the final word."

I love that idea: *Just keep reading.*

Surgery

Surgery began at approximately 12:45 p.m. and lasted almost five hours. The surgeons cut through my scalp to reach my skull, making an incision that started at my forehead hairline, going straight back to the crown of my scalp, then wrapping to the back of my left ear.

Only a one-inch-wide path on my scalp that marked the location of the incision needed to be shaved. On pulling back my scalp, one of the surgical team members removed a disc-shaped section of my skull so that they could gain access to the tumor site.

Because the mass had grown so large and had pressed onto the skull with such a tremendous force, the tumor had adhered to both my brain and my skull. They removed a small amount of brain

117

matter and skull bone as they excised the tumor. With a titanium plate in the shape of a manhole cover, the surgeons replaced the section of removed bone and fastened to the outlying area of my skull with titanium pins. Although the surgery had been quite intrusive, I was left relatively intact.

Now we needed to see what would happen in recovery.

Grace isn't always easy.

Grace Can Be Hard

A time will come in your struggle when you're emotionally spent. You'll want it to be over. You'll be ready to tap out. The cancer isn't going away. The relationship isn't mending. Your cupboards are bare. You have no money to fill them. You think you're at the end of your rope ... but are you really? What if you're at a comma, not a period? Sir Winston Churchill said, "Never, never, never-never give up." Journalist Germany Kent said, "Never give up ... stop worrying and start trusting God. It will be worth it." Is it that simple?

Simple? Yes. Easy? Not on your life.

This is a time to steer clear of platitudes.[20] When someone pats your shoulder and says God's grace can work everything out for good, the comment seems at best a bit naïve and at worst extremely offensive.

I think even God cringes over empty perkiness. But Scripture says, "We know God works for the good of those who love him" (Romans 8:28 NIV). That's different.

There are several "we know" phrases in Romans 8. I'm not much of a Greek scholar, but I love when words pull thoughts together. The Greek word for "we know" means unshakable confidence, absolute. We also see it in verse 22: "We know that the whole creation has been groaning as in the pains of childbirth right up to the present time."

---

20   Is there ever a good time, other than word games with your friends, that platitudes are good?

Paul is trying to tell us gently but resolutely:

1. Life gets tough (v. 22)
2. God is good (v. 28)

And His words are absolutely true. That's the promise of grace. But it's a struggle when you're dealing with an unfavorable diagnosis, your marriage is falling apart, you just picked your child up from jail, or your finances are in the toilet.

Faux-Grace

I grew up in a small town in the Midwest where if I hurt someone's feelings or was disrespectful to an adult, it was my obligation to make it right. That usually included grunting an *I'm sorry* to my friends or the same grunt wrapped with a ma'am or sir for the adult. It made sense to teach children this principle, but, unfortunately, the way I internalized it was flawed and set me on a path of seeing forgiveness and grace contrary to how God designed it. I grew up thinking that when someone hurt me, forgiveness happened when they said "I'm sorry." If they didn't say it, I didn't forgive.

That's not how forgiveness works. That's not grace.

Let's be honest. When someone hurts you down to the quick—down to your soul—are there any words that can make such an intense pain go away? Of course not! There are some pains words can't touch.

But in those terrible moments of pain, allow yourself to smile, because that's exactly where you were when God extended grace to you through Jesus. There were no words you could say to make it right with God. It took Him sacrificing His own son for your behalf.

A relationship with Jesus cancels your debt.[44] And it wasn't earned. It was free. A gift from God and His Son, directly to you.

Now *that's* grace.

Serendipitous Effects

Offering grace in a painful situation can bring confidence. Just as gratitude is a change in attitude, so is our reasoning with grace. Instead of asking "What is the reason for this?" try asking "What is His *purpose* for this?" It doesn't change the situation, but it changes the approach from *because* to *for*.

Remember what the response was when Jesus came across a man who had been born blind (John 9)? Why did this happen? Whose sin caused it? We want an explanation. But Jesus steered us away from the question and instructs us to look at the situation differently. Jesus said that these things happened so the works of God's hands could be displayed.

The country was riveted to the story of Bothem Jean, a 26-year-old accountant who was shot and killed by Amber Guyger, a white Dallas police officer who said she mistook his apartment for her own. During the trial, she readily confessed that she shot Jean because, after returning home from work, she entered his apartment thinking it was hers. Seeing him there, she thought he was an intruder and shot him.

The story is tragic, but what resonated after the guilty verdict and ten-year sentence for Guyger was Bothem's brother, Brandt Jean, who offered complete forgiveness:

> "I love you just like anyone else, and I'm not gonna say I hope you rot and die just like my brother did, but I personally want the best for you. I wasn't gonna ever say this in front of my family or anyone, but I don't even want you to go to jail. I want the best for you because I know that's exactly what Botham would want you to do and the best would be, give your life to Christ ... Again, I love you as a person and I don't wish anything bad on you."

After delivering his statement, Brandt then asked the judge whether he could rise from his seat and give Guyger a hug. With the judge's approval, he made his way down from the stand as Guyger rushed to embrace him.[45]

As I watched the exchange between two people, forever tied by tragedy, I saw a hurting man offer grace to the one most undeserving. The judge cried. The bailiff was heard crying. The act of unfettered grace gripped the country for days.

Getting what we deserve has nothing to do with grace. And I'm thankful every day that it doesn't.

Can you look at your worst with confidence that God, in His grace, always has a purpose, and that this situation is an opportunity to allow His glory to shine? If you can approach what's happening with you in this way, your heart will lighten. Your smile will return. Your purpose will be clear.

Think about it. Ponder. Weigh it out against what you've learned from the exercises in this book. Grace is awesome when received. And grace is healing when given.

What You Can Know

God's grace is never an accident. It always has a purpose.

When grace offered is contingent on how the receiver responds or reacts, it's no longer grace. It's a barter or payment. When Jesus offers grace, He does so freely, not waiting for repayment. This is how we can emulate Christ-like behavior. When we offer grace, we voluntarily take on the effects of the affront made. When we offer grace, the person who hurts us doesn't shake off the effects, we take on the effects with them.

It's not fair. And it doesn't seem right. But it's what Jesus did.

Not long ago I was talking with a girl friend who shared that her husband was struggling with an addiction to pornography. I wanted to weep at the beauty of her words. "I was really angry when he first told me about the porn. But after a day of crying and praying, I realized we were married—a team—and we needed to face this head on. He has work and counseling to do. But he's not doing it alone. I'm right there with him. Because we are one, and I carry his burdens like he carries mine."

God's grace is never an accident. It always has a purpose. And we need to be purposeful with our grace as well.

Read the words written by Apostle Paul in 1 Corinthians 15. This man wrote much of the New Testament, yet he understood the beauty of receiving grace from others, "For I am the least of the apostles and do not even deserve to be called an apostle, because I persecuted the church of God. But by the grace of God I am what I am, and his grace to me was not without effect. No, I worked harder than all of them—yet not I, but the grace of God that was with me" (1 Corinthians 15:9-10).

A Story of Celebration

In researching for this book, I came across Craig Merimee's blog,[46] and his February 29, 2012 entry was most moving. Craig was dealing with pancreatic cancer. His last entry broke my heart:

> "Just looking at myself in the mirror, I can tell my downward spiral has begun. I'm at my all-time low of about 118 pounds. I have an awkward time shaving my face because it is pure bone, and I feel like I'm having to shave to every bony contour my face has. My yellow eyes constantly remind me my jaundice is settling back in. This pretty much means things are going to eventually start shutting down. There's nothing out there that makes sense for me to do to treat this that we haven't already looked at yet ...
>
> The encouragement I have that my eternal life will be in Heaven and that I will be cancer free soon puts a smile on my face ...

I am very motivated about [w]hat the future has to
offer me that there is a lot of reason to be excited
...."

I came to the end of his post ... *God is good!* Oh, please, friend.
Know without a doubt that God is good. He's in your corner.
Never give up.

UNDER THE UMBRELLA

How have your life's complications made you a better person? Or do you think they haven't?

_____

_____

_____

_____

_____

_____

_____

_____

_____

_____

_____

_____

_____

_____

_____

_____

_____

_____

_____

_____

Chapter Twelve

Now What?

Journal entry: Saturday, April 16, 2011, 2:19 p.m.

I'm thrilled to be alive and at home. I'm one blessed gal.

The Morning's Prayer of Uncertainty

*Father, I don't understand any of this. Your presence
is all-encompassing. You brought me through surgery,
but now what?*

The first few days after leaving the hospital were filled with
surprises and challenges. Normalcy skirted the outside corners
of my life. My face, neck, and even chest were still covered with
bruises due to the five-hour surgery. My balance and control over
the muscles on the right side of my body were compromised. But I
knew I was healing. I took the time to relax and reflect. A seizure,

a brain tumor, immediate surgery, survival, and acceptance of possible limitations.

But now what do I do?

Like me, you may be facing the *now what* phase of your worst time ever. Are you looking for comfort, relief, or escape?

For me, it was Scripture. I was hungry for a purpose, and Scripture took on a new priority in my life. Hear the beauty, comfort, and promise in Isaiah 40:28-31:

> "Do you not know? Have you not heard? The Lord is the everlasting God, the Creator of the ends of the earth. He does not tired or weary and His understanding no one can fathom. He gives strength to the weary, and increases the power of the weak. Even youths grow tired and weary, and young men stumble and fall; but those who hope in the Lord will renew their strength. They will soar on wings like eagles; they will run and not grow weary; they will walk and not be faint" (NIV).

The Next Right Step

If you have read each chapter and followed each of its suggestions, I applaud you for seeking healing.

The purpose of this chapter is to help when the dust settles. When you have allowed God to lead you through victory and you've decided your victory is a life filled with seeking God's intent.

Sadly, this is a broken world and terrible things happen in it. Children are sexually abused, wives are beaten, women lose battles with breast cancer, and men lose jobs and struggle to find new ones. Unfortunately, the list is long with all the wrongs that can happen. But when we allow Christ to guide our life, hope and healing is extended to us. Maybe the bills are still outstanding or ramifications from bad choices are still being felt. Or maybe the diagnosis from the doctor hasn't matched prayers offered. Yet, in spite of it all, you stand victorious, because you have met tragedy face-to-face and have not looked away. Instead, you've chosen to stand behind your Savior, allowing Him to fight your battle. You've taken His lead, stared into the eye of evil, and haven't blinked.

You have turned this battle over and are now looking for what your role should be.

The tragedy may still be around you, but your victory is real. Embrace your new vision of life.

The Importance of "I Love You"

I experienced how life can change in a moment. Tragedy can do that to a person. Dealing with a brain tumor has taught me many lessons. First and foremost, don't leave words unspoken. Tell your friends and family that you love them. And then love them—unconditionally. You may need to find the proper boundaries for those who don't always want what's best for you, but love them where they are.

Jesus taught his disciples that nothing was more powerful than love. The love that God has for His Son, the love Jesus had for the world's sinners, and the love we all need to share with one another:

> "Love your enemies, do good to those who hate you, bless those who curse you, pray for those who mistreat you. If someone slaps you on one cheek, turn to them the other also. If someone takes your coat, do not withhold your shirt from them. Give to everyone who asks you, and if anyone takes what belongs to you, do not demand it back. Do to others as you would have them do to you. If you love those who love you, what credit is that to you? Even sinners love those who love them. And if you do good to those who are good to you, what credit is that to you? Even sinners do that. And if you lend to those from whom you expect repayment, what credit is that to you? Even sinners lend to sinners, expecting to be repaid in full. But love

your enemies, do good to them, and lend to them without expecting to get anything back. Then your reward will be great, and you will be children of the Most High, because he is kind to the ungrateful and wicked" (Luke 6:27-35 NIV).

A world can be changed when love is offered. Never hold it back.

Daily Challenges

When people hear about my physical battle with a brain tumor, many are quick to ask if I have a scar. I smile and say yes, and I'm very proud of it. My is scar an outward sign of the battle I waged over meningioma.[21] I celebrate my scar. And I have come to appreciate and be thankful for the opportunities that stem from the tumor. Your challenge is to celebrate your worst as well.

"Affliction is the best book in my library,"[47] is one of Martin Luther's most quoted sayings. In other words, pain redeemed speaks louder than pain removed. While we're concerned with how things turn out, God is most concerned with how *we* turn out. Coming through a crisis, we can use our faith to catapult us to a more intimate relationship with Christ.

Take a deep breath. You've now experienced your worst. You've stepped beyond healing and hearing about a relationship with God. You've put in the work to rid yourself of all your distractions and are truly experiencing what God has in store for you.

Even if the news isn't what you wanted.

Returning to Habakkuk, we see an amazing example of a person's response to receiving the worst news he could ever receive. His response is healthy and balanced. He obeys by listening to God (Chapter 2), ponders over God's faithfulness of the past (3:3-15), and then waits patiently for His answer. He then encourages himself

---

21   The name of my type of tumor.

and others in the hope he receives and understands through his expressed faith (3:16-19). He wrote it down for others who would follow to be comforted as they worship God.

We're instructed to encourage others as well. In 2 Corinthians, Apostle Paul shares why living beyond our own worst has value: "Praise be to the God and Father of our Lord Jesus Christ, the Father of compassion and the God of all comfort, who comforts us in all our troubles, so that we can comfort those in any trouble with the comfort we ourselves receive from God. For just as we share abundantly in the sufferings of Christ, so also our comfort abounds through Christ" (2 Corinthians 3-5 NIV).

Did you ever think one day you would be offering comfort and wisdom to someone dealing with what you've just come through?

Getting There

But where do you start? You want to continue getting closer to God. You want to be available to help others to get through what you've battled. But it sounds a bit daunting.

It's just like a beaver building a dam: he uses one stick at a time until the job is finished.

☑ Keep a journal. Write about your journey. Your fears. Your victories. You've started already in this book. Keep it going. You will enjoy revisiting your scribbles and seeing where God has continued to stay by your side. If you choose to dig deeper into your healing journey, *God's Best During Your Worst: A Guided Journal* is available.

☑ Pray and make your conversations with God tangible. Write your prayers—your requests as well as your praises. Post around the house little reminders of your requests and the answers you've received.

☑ Continue to read Scripture daily. Don't be fooled. Satan still sees a target on your back. Write uplifting verses on a

129

card and carry them in your pocket or create memes for your social media.

☑ Be proud of any scar you may have that is associated with your worst. It's a sign of victory. Respect it. Honor it. It didn't come cheaply. You earned it. Remember, anyone who has gone through a ferocious battle retains scars.

Progress and Setback

While I made progress after surgery, I also dealt with fears and setbacks.

I made Lew stay right outside the bathroom door when I began taking showers. That way, if I fell, he would hear and know to come in and help. He was patient and kind with me. He stayed close until I felt confident in my ability to stay safe.

Maybe your marriage was almost decimated by adultery. But you and your spouse are dedicated to accepting God's direction and restoring what has been devastated. Be honest with one another if it's scary to trust again. Healing needs honesty to continue. Find that sweet spot of "trust but verify."

Even those who have suffered pain beyond belief find their way through setbacks and struggles. In 1975, author Paula D'Arcy lost her husband and twenty-one-month-old daughter in a car crash involving a drunk driver. She has since led grief groups after major catastrophes such as Hurricane Katrina.

> "'I realized that there are two levels of life,' she said in reflecting on her own grief. 'One is the small story of your life and the other is the movement of the spirit of God trying to help our souls awaken to the power greater than anything that will ever happen to us. Grief was the opening through which I found that power. In many ways, it was a great gift to be broken open at so young an age because it gave me the rest of my life to benefit from what I'd learned … No matter what else might happen,

130

I'd found a place inside that is greater than the darkness.'"[48]

The Ultimate of Healing

In Jerry Sittser's book, *A Grace Revealed*, he admits he cannot end his story of finding grace like one can end a children's story, with a bow and *happily ever after* ending.

"Eventually, we will live happily ever after, but only when the redemptive story ends, which seems like a long way off. In the meantime, you and I are somewhere in the middle of the story, as if stuck in the chaos and messiness of a half-finished home improvement project. We might have one chapter left in our story, or we might have fifty. We could experience more of the same for years to come or we could be on the verge of a change so dramatic that if we knew about it we would faint with fear or wonder, or perhaps both. We could be entering in the happiest phase of our lives, or the saddest. We simply don't know and can't know …

In my mind there is only one good option: we must choose to stay in the redemptive story. However unclear it might be to us, we can trust that God is writing the story."[49]

It's my hope that you see yourself in the middle of your story. If you need to use the tools we covered earlier, do not hesitate to do so. Set your timer for thirty minutes, and when it rings, thank God for holding you safe in the middle of your story, and ask Him to carry you through to the end.

Closing Thoughts

This has been quite a journey we've taken together, you and me. You had the courage to pick up this book and consider that, just maybe, there was an answer to how to live life beyond your tragedy. I am humbled that you trusted me as you continued to turn each page. Perhaps you threw the book across the room a time or two. Doesn't matter. You picked it back up again and continued on. I applaud you for that.

I don't know what your worst was. I don't know what you're going through, what feelings you've buried, or what you've already survived. But I know this: God loves us enough to watch His perfect Son die for our sin-riddled lives. He offered the greatest gift possible so we could know and glorify Him while we're here on earth. And when we leave here, we can spend eternity in heaven with Him.

He loves us that much. And Scripture tells us we're able to love Him—or anyone else for that matter—because He showed us how: "We love because he first loved us" (1 John 4:19).

I'm truly sorry we met under these circumstances. But be encouraged that the spark of hope inside you hasn't died. Like the father of the son possessed who prayed and asked God to help him believe ... like Habakkuk, who asked difficult questions and was prepared to hear God's response ... you can look forward and know that God is there, no matter the outcome.

I don't have all the answers to the difficult questions you may ask. But after experiencing my worst-ever moment, I watched God move in miraculous ways. I have taken the time to review dark periods in my life and have seen God's hand everywhere. I know, without a doubt, that my yesterdays prove to me that my tomorrows are firmly planted in my heavenly Father's hand. I hope you can experience the same peace and assuredness.

If not today, perhaps tomorrow.

UNDER THE UMBRELLA

Between you and God, what would it take to convince you that He loves you and is for you?

_____

_____

_____

_____

_____

_____

_____

_____

_____

_____

_____

_____

_____

_____

_____

_____

_____

_____

Chapter Thirteen

Lived Promises: God at His Best

*M*y brain tumor blessed my life. I only shared bits and pieces of my ten-day journey with you. Primarily because this book isn't about me. It's about God's grace and the relentless love He has for us all.

Can't see it yet? I get it.

This book is to give you hope. Maybe you found these examples entertaining, but they never resonated with you.

I understand skepticism.

But what if you heard from others ... in their own words?

Letting God Fight the Battles

Sometimes we think our struggles are beyond God's help. He may be big, but not big enough. Read how Donna Brown's choices turned her world upside down, leaving her with no hope. But God was there to see her through.

> As a teen, I fell in love with Kevin, a bad-boy from high school, which worked fine since I wasn't so squeaky-clean myself. After a time together, I became pregnant, so we immediately got married.

We thought life would be perfect. That was, until we went out with some friends.

After drinking only a few beers, we slipped right back into a partying lifestyle. Our marriage took a back seat to my husband's partying life. He started spending more time at the bars after work with his buddies. When he was home, we'd fight about his drinking. I was tormented with loneliness, jealousy, and uncertainty.

I thought if I'd join him—drink and party as hard as he did—maybe I would feel like a part of his life again. We went to a party together, and I danced with all the different guys there. I loved the attention and felt pretty again. All the while, my husband held up the bar with his buddies as he talked with other women.

The next morning, God began talking to my heart, and days later I knelt in our living room and prayed. Through tears and heartache, I asked Jesus to forgive me and cleanse me of my sin. There in my living room, I made Jesus Christ Lord of my life.

I shared my faith with my husband, and he thought I was crazy. He wanted us to have fun drinking, but I wanted to live for Jesus. I stopped all partying and began going to church. I tried to be the wife Christ wanted me to be, but my husband tore me and my faith down every chance he had, telling me my Christianity wasn't real.

Yet I fell deeper in love with Jesus. Scripture comforted me; "The eyes of the Lord watch over those who do right; his ears are open to their cries for help" (Psalm 34:15).

I prayed every day for my husband, for myself,

and that I would know what to say to this man, whom I loved, but tormented me continually. For Christmas I bought him a Bible, only to have him look at it and say, "A Bible? Why'd you waste your money on this for me?" and watch him toss it across the room.

He continually belittled me, but I continued to pray, clinging to God's promises. But I wondered if even God could break his heart.

As our routine, I'd ask my husband to join me at church and he'd refuse, wanting me to stay home with him instead. But one morning I responded, "Don't make me choose between you and God. The choice has already been made. And I chose God first." I continued getting my daughter and me ready for the morning services. I went to the car and was loading my daughter into her car seat when I turned and saw my husband running toward the car, all disheveled.

"I—I decided to come today."

When we pulled into the church parking lot, he got out of the car and headed in without me. After getting our girl settled in the nursery, I entered the sanctuary and found him sitting in the third row from the front, head in his hands.

I scooted in beside him. "Are you okay?"

"God said 'Last call, Donn.' He said, 'Last call.' I'm a drunk. That's how you get a drunk's attention."

At the end of the service, the pastor asked all who wanted to make a commitment to Jesus to come to the front. My husband jumped out of the pew before the man finished speaking.

That was forty years ago.

He often tells that story—from the pulpit of the church he pastors.

He has dedicated his life to serving God and to two of his greatest loves in ministry—leading hurting people to Christ and helping heal marriages.

Yes, God was big enough. He fought the battle for me. Oh, how I praise Him.

For Our Good and His Glory

Fran Sandin shared with me the pain that comes from losing a child.

My husband, Jim, had just begun his medical practice, and I was busy as his part-time office nurse and mom of our three children. Following a recent spiritual renewal, the Holy Spirit whispered to me: "You will be going through a dark valley, but don't be afraid. I will be with you." Everything in our family seemed great, and I couldn't understand the warning.

A few days later, our seventeen-month-old son, Jeffrey, awoke on a Sunday morning with a fever. Jim took both our other children, Steve, 5, and Angie, 3, to church while I took care of Jeffrey at home. When I called the pediatrician, he noted that many children were sick with a short-term virus, so I was sure we'd wait it out and carry on with life once his fever broke.

But Jeffrey's condition worsened.

Later that day, Jim and I took him to the ER, where a spinal tap confirmed bacterial meningi-

138

tis—a severe case that we would soon learn would not respond to the latest antibiotics or state-of-the-art medical management.

Sadly, we said good-bye to our baby on Thursday of the same week. We were all shocked and emotionally devastated. Even through my tears, I remembered the Lord's words shared in Scripture: "I will never desert you nor will I ever forsake you;" [22] "My peace I give you, not as the world gives do I give to you;" [23] and "My grace is sufficient for you." [24]

Even though God's words echoed in my heart, I still had questions—many questions.

Is the Lord punishing me?

How can I conquer fear?

Does God answer prayer?

Will I ever get over this?

Am I becoming bitter?

How can God use this experience for good?

I knew I couldn't function like this. To regain sanity, I had to seek truth. I sought God like never before. And He met me. As I meditated on the specialness of Jeffrey, God, through the Holy Spirit, brought to mind the sweetness of Psalm 139. He knew Jeffrey's life from beginning to its end. [25]

Through several years of Bible study and divinely appointed encounters with both written and spoken words, my heart healed. I used my newfound purpose and launched a writing career

---

22   Hebrews 13:5 (NASB)
23   John 14:27 (NASB)
24   2 Corinthians 12:9 (NASB)
25   Job 14:5

with the desire to help others. My book, *See You Later, Jeffrey*, was published eleven years after I first began writing it. Since then, it has been translated into different languages. Jim and I have been blessed to share over 2,000 copies of this book in the Ukraine and Germany.

When Jeffrey was in the ICU, Jim and I knelt in the soft light of the children's hospital chapel, where we held hands as Jim prayed, "Dear Lord, we give Jeffrey back to you and we pray You will use this experience for our good and for Your glory!"

Since Jeffrey's death all those years ago, Jim and I have felt doubly blessed: once to have had the pleasure of experiencing seventeen months with such a beautiful little boy, and second, to have the reassurance that we will see him again.

The memory of Jeffrey is imprinted in our hearts. While our arms were empty for a time, we confidently look forward to holding and hugging him for all eternity. Glory to God.

A Menacing Darkness

Joanna [fictitious name] was quick to share her story about considering suicide when she faced her worst:

My life was out of control, running from one relationship to another. I had tried everything under the sun to control my world and had failed miserably at each attempt. I finally married, settling for a man who wasn't right for me, but hoping for the best.

One evening, when my husband was away on a business trip and the kids were all tucked safely in their beds, Evil paid me a visit.

His voice hissed. "Nothing about you is good. Everything you are is dirty and vile."

Acrid smells filled the room. I looked around but saw nothing.

He continued. "You're such a waste of a life. A useless mother. Your kids would be better off without you."

My thoughts raced. No! You have to stop! Go away!

I didn't want to listen, but the words began making sense.

"I can make your pain go away. It's not that big of a deal. You can stop hurting. All you need to do is go into the garage and turn on the car. Finish it off. It's so simple."

Sweat dampened my hair as I lay in bed and continued to cradle the pillow around my head. My heartbeat raced. Pain tightened my chest.

"Nobody will ever love you because you don't have what it takes."

I began sobbing in defeat. Nobody wanted me, except Evil. I knew he spoke in lies, but I couldn't fight his words any longer.

He was right. I would be better off dead. Everyone would be better off. This is the best solution for a problem like me.

Sighing, I pushed back the covers and slowly sat up. Pulling my hair back and off my tear-streaked face, I gathered my thoughts. I lowered my feet to the floor. This was it.

I looked around. Where's my purse? I need to find my keys. I'll go into the garage, turn on the car, and never wake up. Let's do this and be done with it. No more pain ever again.

Standing in the middle of my bedroom with tears running down my cheeks, I was completely broken. Yet I turned to God. In a despondent voice, I whimpered, "God, help me."

I hadn't expected a miracle.

Miracles were for the people God loved. I couldn't expect Him to really love me after all my messes. Yet in that moment—the moment I called out, broken and helpless, to God—I felt a complete sense of warmth that started in the depths of my heart and exploded through my entire body. I sensed heaven's floodgates open as peace washed over me and sucked all remnants of evil from the room. Standing there, emotionally and physically exhausted, I felt myself being pulled into the arms of an unseen presence that embraced me as a parent consoles a child. Warm and secure. Leaning into these invisible arms, I began to sob.

"Oh, God. Oh, God."

In that moment, everything seemed so clear. God, in fact, did love me and had loved me all along. And I realized something just as powerful: Evil did not have authority over me.

I sensed a voice—a sweet voice—in my spirit.

"Read the book of James."

Dropping my keys and purse, I reached for the Bible from the nightstand. I sat on the edge of my bed and, with quivering fingers, searched for the Book of James. Once I found the right page, I took a deep breath and began to read.

"Consider it pure joy, my brothers and sisters, whenever you face trials of many kinds, because you know that the testing of your faith produces perseverance. Let perseverance finish its work so that you may be mature and complete, not lacking anything. If any of you lacks wisdom, you should ask God, who gives generously to all without finding fault, and it will be given to you." [26]

In that instant, I had finally found what I had longed for—an acceptance from God. When I called to Him, He saved me. We were in a relationship, God and me. He wanted to know me, love me, and have me love Him. Not from duty, but with a praising and trusting heart. My life was changed by God's unfailing love.

A Lifetime of Guilt Forgiven

Sandra [fictitious name] had let unforgiveness and guilt control her life for over thirty years. It wasn't until God healed her heart that she was truly set free.

I didn't have a care in the world. I was eighteen years old and in love and engaged. The love of my life had promised to love me forever. That's why I went further than I wanted to when we parked. But he loved me. He'd said so.

But it was all lies.

Then I found out I was pregnant.

I was raised Catholic. Things like this never happened to people like me.

---

26   James 1:2-5 (NIV)

Abortion. I couldn't even say the word. I wanted to die. I thought I could kill myself, but I couldn't do that either. Catholics don't commit suicide.

Or murder.

I was alone in this.

I went to the nearest pregnancy center to get answers. They told me they understood.

"Girls have abortions all the time. It won't hurt, and, besides, it's not a baby. It's just a bunch of cells."

Her voice was so soothing. If I went through with the procedure—that's what she called it, a procedure—I wouldn't have to tell anyone. Life would get better, and I would be okay.

So I did it.

But life didn't get better. I wasn't okay.

Now, not only was I a murderer, I was a liar for life. I couldn't even confess, especially to the priest. My secret stopped me from asking God for forgiveness.

I couldn't forgive myself.

Years passed, and I met another man who said he'd love me forever too. But this time I waited for sex until we were married. I thought then I'd have my happily-ever-after. And I was happy ... for a while. I even got pregnant again. God must have forgiven me.

After my Emily was born, I breathed a sigh of relief. Life would be perfect now.

But it still wasn't.

Guilt haunted me. I cried on the anniversary of

my horrid decision. My marriage suffered. I never wanted to keep secrets from him, but he was a good Catholic. How could he ever look at me if he knew what I had done? When we went to Mass and celebrated the Eucharist, I knew I was lying.

Always more lies.

I wanted to die. I thought about dying a lot. Not because I hated life, but I hated all the pain and deception I was living.

It shouldn't have been a surprise that my marriage ended. My relationship with my daughter suffered as well.

I had made a terrible choice that cost the life of my own baby—I had decided she was a girl—and it haunted me every day. I was totally unlovable. God couldn't even love me.

Then a friend asked me to come to her church. She was sweet, and I knew if I went once, I could tell her no the next time.

But her church was different. People smiled ... said they were happy to see me ... and hoped I'd come back again. When the service started and the preacher began speaking, I wanted to cry. "This is not about religion, folks. It's about falling in love with a Savior who loves you, no matter how bad you think you are."

Even a murderer?

I came back again, and again, and again. Soon their love began to break down the walls around my heart. That was when I felt the need to unburden myself of my secret. I pulled one of the nice women aside and risked sharing my dark story. After years of carrying such a heavy load, it was time to rid myself of secrets and guilt.

Through tears, I told her what I had done. And you know what she did? She told me that Jesus loved me, and His death was to free me of my torment. That He longed for a relationship with me. It wasn't about religion or trying to be perfect, it was about a relationship.

"Sandra, all have sinned and fallen short of the glory of God, but it doesn't stop there. The Bible also says we are all justified freely by his grace through the redemption that came by Christ Jesus.[27] That means He can even forgive you."

Even me.

I no longer live under the cloud of shame, I live under the blessing of Grace. I still think about my baby ... my girl ... and smile, looking forward to our first hug.

Learning to Trust and Wait on God

My British friend Sharon Tedford shares how starting a family was what she desired, but it wasn't as easy as she thought. Getting pregnant was never her problem—staying pregnant was.

Before our first son was born, we had two miscarriages, and I was left shaken. I was young and healthy, never imagining I would experience this pain and devastation not once, but twice. After the second miscarriage, my husband and I met with our doctor, a wonderfully compassionate woman, and she encouraged us to rest. Take a break. Let our hearts heal. After a few months, maybe try again.

---

27   Romans 3:23-24

Try again. It seemed so simple.

When the time came for a third pregnancy test and it came back positive, I began to experience the dread of "what if."

What if we lost this baby too?

What if I had done something wrong with both other pregnancies?

What if I failed again?

What if? What if?

One Friday morning, in those delicate first weeks, I started to experience symptoms of miscarrying. I went straight to my general practitioner, who tried to make me an appointment at the maternity ward (women's hospital), but the next emergency appointment wasn't until first thing Monday morning.

My doctor and I were both frustrated. And scared.

As I laid on the examining table, my tears ran over my cheeks and soaked my pillow. She did her best to reassure me. She attempted to find the baby's heartbeat, but it was too early for her unsophisticated equipment to hear it. I could tell she didn't want to raise my hopes too high. But I could also tell that she was praying as she tried.

She passed the fetal Doppler over my abdomen, stopping here—then there—searching for a baby's heartbeat. My heartbeat was clearly audible, but there was no sign of the baby's.

Nothing.

She tried again over to the right. Nothing.

Lower. Again, nothing.

Only the strong beat of my own heartbeat, as if calling for another to answer it.

Suddenly the doctor stopped. She cocked her head and squinted ... pushed on the Doppler a bit harder.

Then she smiled.

And there it was. The tiny, racing rhythm came calling, pushing through the fog and dancing in our ears. Not only was there a baby, but it had a healthy heartbeat.

My doctor shed her own tears then.

"In all my years, I have never found a heartbeat on such a tiny baby. This is a miracle!"

As I sat in front of her at her desk and sobbed away all the trepidation I had gathered, she told me to keep my Monday appointment at the women's hospital. They would want to do further tests and a scan.

After I left her office, time passed at a snail's pace waiting for my Monday appointment. Saturday folded into Sunday. The church service that morning was pretty much a write-off. I took up space in the pew, but I didn't want to be there. I was wrapped in anxiety.

When the pastor preached about the blessings found in waiting, his words penetrated the walls I had built around my heart. I realized I needed God to help me wait again to see if this child would be born into our arms or straight into His. The pastor read: "You will not have to fight this battle. Take up your positions; stand firm and see the deliverance the Lord will give you, O Judah and Jerusalem. Do not be afraid; do not be discouraged. Go out and face them tomorrow and the Lord will be with you." [28]

As I sat in church, I was wrapped in the worst fear I'd ever experienced, and, in that moment, God gave me the best hope I could ask for. He gave me His best during my worst.

If I knew then what I know now, I'd have skipped into the Monday morning appointment at the hospital. That tiny baby is now our adult son, a young man who loves Jesus and serves people. But if I had not experienced that terrible fear, I would never have known extraordinary faith in a God who delivers His promises.

I thank God for those two babies who we will one day meet in the presence of Jesus. I thank God for the struggle to stay pregnant. I am grateful for the three children God placed into our arms through the miracle of birth. I am thankful for every moment of doubt, for every day filled with shaky faith, and every prayer lifted through the pain of uncertainty.

Learning to trust God was a journey, but so worth the effort.

Trusting God to Change His Mind

We know that God created the universe and set the East apart from the West. Scripture tells us of all the miracles, from parting the Red Sea (Exodus 14) ... to making the sun stand still (Joshua 10) ... to Jesus rising from the grave (Luke 24). But does God ever change His mind? Read Christina Custodio's story of how that happened.

---

28   2 Chronicles 20:17 (NIV)

I felt like I was in a nightmare the night of September 8, 2015. It was a total "out-of-body" experience. The middle school's football trainer called and said that my thirteen-year-old son Isaiah had a headache and he needed to be picked up from practice.

It started as just a headache.

Ever since Isaiah was born, I felt God was going to take him from me. I know it sounds strange, but it's just something I felt. So when we were later told that he had bleeding on the brain (diagnosed as a ruptured arterio vascular malformation) and it was really bad, I knew the day I most feared had come.

I left the waiting room, where friends and family were surrounding my husband Ozzy and me with love and prayers, and walked into the bathroom. I wasn't crying. I wasn't hysterical. I was just scared. My legs were shaking. Sitting there all alone, I begged and pleaded with God not to take my son. He's only 13! Seriously? You're going to take him now?

I recalled scriptures that told about God changing his mind (Exodus 34, Jonah 3), and that gave me the audacity to begged Him to change His mind for my family. On that seat, alone in the hospital restroom, I prayed, *Change your mind, change your mind, change your mind.*

The surgeon began cutting into his skull at 11:12 pm. September 8th. I pictured Ozzy's mom, who had died three years earlier, waiting at the gates to take Isaiah's hand and lead him home.

I wasn't being a pessimist. I wasn't being overly dramatic. I wasn't being a crazy, emotional mother. I knew God was going to take him. I just ... knew it. I've always been aware that my children are on loan. From day one, I dedicated them to God, knowing that they were His.

I came out of the bathroom, sat back down on the couch, and began picturing my son's funeral, and how I would tell the girls, and how I would survive, and wondering if my marriage could take this kind of blow. Although, I was afraid of having to deal with that kind of reality, I still had a crazy kind of peace. It was truly mind blowing, but I knew if God decided to go ahead and take him, I would survive. I would be okay, and I could even thrive. It was an absolutely miraculous feeling and reaction to a scenario that I could never imagine stepping into with any kind of peace or grace. But it was in my face, and I knew we would all be okay.

Yet I still begged for my son's life.

God heard my prayer and the prayers of the thirty-two others standing with Ozzy and me in that room. He heard the prayers of the youth group after their leader sent out a message telling them to stop whatever they were doing and pray. He heard each and every one of us.

And He changed His mind.

I really don't know how to explain what that really means, but I know that's what happened. From the moment I felt and knew that He would save Isaiah, the blessings over the situation began.

What began as the worst thing ever turned into one of my greatest blessings. There has been blessing after blessing every single day throughout this whole ordeal. I can honestly say that, though challenging, these are some of the best times I have had in my life. Seeing God's grace, mercy, and overall awesomeness each and every day we are here is incredible.

Even though our lives were turned upside down, God's grace continued to cover us.

More Stories Waiting to be Told
Each story I've shared was birthed from life-changing devastation. Yet God was there, waiting for them to reach out to Him. And more stories are out there, ready to be told. Will one be yours? It's my prayer that you reach out to God, too. Let Him heal your heart. He's big enough and He wants to pull you close. But He's waiting for an invitation from you.

Allow God to shine in your life. Stand back, and watch God give you His best during your worst.

God *is* Trustworthy

*I*have been so powerfully humbled by all of the happenings since my seizure on April 1, 2011, the worst day of my life. I still sit back and marvel at how my life changed so drastically over such a short period of time.

Lessons Learned Along the Way

Since April 11, I have learned the merit of waiting and taking in what's all around so I can heal and continue to lean on God. While time does not heal all wounds, we can be His hands and feet, helping others through their worst times (Romans 12:13). God has given you gifts to do that, too. If you are good with your hands, help with rebuilding what has been torn down. If you're a good listener, help by listening to those who are hurting. And as Christ followers, we all have the capacity to love. If someone is alone, we can love them along in their struggles.

One of the purest blessings through my worst was seeing the difference between need and want. While I discovered my wants far outnumbered my needs, Christ staying close was my only true need.. Listening to my husband sleep restfully after he tended to my needs for a long day was a fulfilled want. So was watching the bruising from surgery fade from a violent red-blue, to a yellowish-green, then to nothing at all. Chatting it up with friends who loved me and wanted to know for themselves that I was getting better was a very welcomed want.

Your worst will bring opportunity to differentiate between your wants and needs as well. That may be difficult to see if you're sitting in the hospital with a hurting child, or while you are with the director of a funeral home preparing for the internment of a parent who committed suicide. All you feel are needs.

You *need* to stop the hurt.

I am so sorry you are hurting right now. God is waiting with you as you get through this. As long as it takes. It is a struggle to find the line between need and want. But you need to know what you know.

Know When to Act

Bonnie and I shared our brain challenge war stories. She with Deep Brain Trauma (DBT) she suffered from a car accident and me from my brain surgery. We discovered we both reacted similarly when friends greeted us after our incident.

You had brain trauma? But you look so good.

Bonnie cringed. "My pastor greeted me at the door after services, raving about how good I looked. I told him if he could take the top of my skull off and look inside, he'd see how scrambled I was. I may look fine, but I'm far from it. Why are people so insensitive?"

The lesson was clear: we don't know what's going on in the lives of others. There may be more pain surrounding them than we can fathom. Look around. Ask God to reveal to you what He sees. Take ten minutes and look around. Try to see what you've missed. Listen to others, and you will see the pain they're hiding. Continue looking away from your own situation and instead, look into the lives of others. You may be surprised at what you find. Following those ten minutes, you will be ready to offer comfort to someone else.

Know When to Speak

We often find ourselves speechless when it comes to offering encouragement. Maybe you can't offer comfort to someone with a brain injury. But if you've suffered a loss through miscarriage, you can offer comfort there. She'll listen to you because you understand. If you can't offer comfort to a woman whose husband walked out on her, maybe your worst has to do with financial devastation. Offer comfort there. If that's her worst, she will listen.

That doesn't mean commiserating with them in their pain. It means offering God's promises in a practical way. It means using your situation as your credibility.

Instead of telling them life will be just fine (you don't know that), you can tell them that they have value and not a second of their pain will be wasted. Soon you will be able to speak with authority, telling them the day will come when there will be no more pain or tears (you do know that). That's the beauty found in brokenness.

In 2 Corinthians 1, the Apostle Paul explained it like this: "God is our merciful Father and the source of all comfort. He comforts us in all our troubles so that we can comfort others. When they are troubled, we will be able to give them the same comfort God has given us" (vv. 3-4 NLT).

My dear friend Michelle Bengtson wrote about her worst:

> "I am so grateful to God to be able to tell you, He has not left me unchanged. That painful experience changed and challenged me in many ways I couldn't have expected. It tested my faith and made me seek truth. It made me confront God on some hard issues. It made me put my trust in God and not in people. And even before the IVs were removed, it gave me a chance to comfort others who were in pain, and really pray for them when I promised I would.
>
> No pain is wasted. God used my pain to help others. And He will use yours in ways you can't even imagine."[50]

Know What You Know

When I was told I may die in ten days, the doctors made sure I had all the medications I needed to prepare for surgery. But I found no peace in medicine. I felt assured the doctors had prepared me the best they could, but peace only came when I reached out to God for help. The circumstances around me didn't change—I was still looking at a possible ten-day death sentence—but His presence gave me the calmness that Apostle Paul wrote about: "And the peace of God, which transcends all understanding, will guard your hearts and your minds in Christ Jesus" (Philippians 4:7 NIV).

I can say with confidence there isn't any argument imaginable that could negate what I learned from my experience. God offered unyielding comfort to me in my pain and never chastised me in my fear.

My brain tumor and period of recovery—which could have been a horrific situation—brought glory to God. It was a chain reaction. Because of a seizure, a humungous brain tumor was found. Because of the tumor, I was given a whisper of time to make sure my priorities were in place. Putting priorities in place, I sought the face of God like never before. I trusted God enough to be as honest as I possibly could with Him. I shared my love and doubt with Him, often experiencing these emotions at the same time. His patience and presence helped me work through the skepticism I had learned at an early age. By staying close, He showed me I was worth it.

Living this side of a miracle is awesome. But it has been the journey I'll remember most—a journey that filled and healed my heart. I have experienced times of great challenges and frustrations since my seizure. My life will forever have a new normal. My goal now is to discover what God intends my normal to be as He allows me to help others in their journey of healing.

And you can live this side of a miracle, too.

What Does This Mean for You?

While I used the discovery of my brain tumor and the subsequent healing process as the vehicle that drove this book, the true focus of it is *your* worst.

What does searching for God's best during your worst mean to *you*? Are you dealing with your own brain-tumor-sized situation? It may be a financial burden that seems to be overwhelming. You may be in the middle of a relationship that is emotionally destroying you and others around you. Are you being abused? Get to a safe place immediately and contact a trusted friend. Whatever it is, God is bigger.

With each day that passes, you can be closer to seeing God's hand in fuller measure. While you may be in what seems the middle of your ordeal, look back and see from where you've come. Have lies and deception rocked your world? Today you're closer to an honest existence than you were yesterday. Was it your choice of having an affair that knocked your world off its axis? While you may be dealing with the consequences of your choices, you're one day closer to living in freedom in an authentic life.

God Cares

On that fateful night as I lay in my hospital bed, I heard God whisper as He had weeks earlier, *Do you trust Me?*

In that moment, God's presence was unmistakable as if I felt His hand on my cheek, His breath brushing against my heart. I didn't know if I would heal to be what I had been before my seizure, if I would die, or if I would land somewhere in between. Yet the peace that filled my hospital room was unquestionable. I knew I'd be fine—whatever happened. I had peace with no guarantee of outcome.

God gave me those ten days to reinvigorate my faith, to pull it apart and look at it from different angles. As my world flashed before me through the variety of feelings that impacted each of the ten days, I saw I could trust in Him.

And if you let Him, He will reinvigorate your faith and trust too.

Nothing ever catches God by surprise. Think about how our loving Heavenly Father agonized over the hardship He knew you would face during this worst. You can be sure He didn't like it, but He was not surprised.

Life-changing peace is more than the absence of pain. It's more than what *isn't*—it's about what *is*. It's about the presence of Jesus Christ.

In *God's Best During Your Worst*, you were asked to unpack a myriad of emotions and viewpoints when facing your worst. Confusion, heartache, and doubt can be difficult perceptions to stare down the first time you try. Other chapters challenged you to consider possibly new vantage points on surrendering to God and offering gratitude. You were pressed to be brutally honest with yourself through the entire process. I hope you were able to see how this change transpired. I hope trust—albeit slowly—came alive for you.

Maybe you had avoided thinking about the source of your pain until picking up *God's Best During Your Worst*. I hope what you read resonated with you. In order to heal, it's inevitable—we all need to take on our demons.

If you're still in the midst of your horrific ordeal, you can find peace in the midst of its torment when you seek a relationship with Jesus Christ. Each chapter of *God's Best During Your Worst* gave examples of how allowing Jesus a place of priority brings that peace. Think of it—as a child of God you are never alone.

He's with you now.

The process of healing began in one decisive moment: when you picked up this book and decided you wanted to find God's best during your worst. By reading this book and journaling as prompted, you took a step of faith and opened those dark corners of your heart. You know the ones … those you thought could never heal.

This journey has not been about trying to answer the question *Why?* because any answer would ring hollow. Instead, consider asking *For what purpose?* I smile on the words Apostle Paul said of himself, "Here is a trustworthy saying that deserves full acceptance: Christ Jesus came into the world to save sinners—of whom I am the worst. But for that very reason I was shown mercy so that in me, the worst of sinners, Christ Jesus might display his immense patience as an example for those who would believe in him and receive eternal life" (1 Timothy 1:15-16 NIV).

I was given mercy in April 2011 so others might see His glory and believe in Jesus. And you were given mercy as well. I hope the journey you took while reading this book was filled with powerful, insightful, and clarifying discoveries. I don't completely understand the peace I experienced during and since brain surgery, but I know it is real.

What about you? I'd love to hear from you. Let me know about your journey. You can reach me at robin@robinluftig.com or on the typical social media sites.

Peace is real, and it's waiting for you, too, if you want it. As I finish this book, I'm praying for you—specifically you. I don't know the hardship you weathered, but I ask God this:

Dear Father,
Please give the reader of this book mercy to withstand what's happened and grace to face what may come. Help him or her see themselves as You see them— loved, known, and accepted. We know we're out of our element in this crisis, but because of what Jesus did on the cross, we are more than okay: we are redeemed. Help the reader take one day at a time and trust that You are in control. And help us all make each step we take bring us closer to You.
In Jesus' name, Amen.

Practicing Gratitude

Writing this book has been an opportunity for me to recall past experiences and try to comprehend the magnitude of some of the blessings I have received during my journey surrounding my brain tumor.

I cannot go on without giving my unabashed love and appreciation to my husband, Lew. God blessed me exponentially when our paths crossed. I watched as his courage overcame fear, his patience knocked out frustrations, and his unyielding trust won over doubt. His complete and unyielding faith in Christ brought light like a beacon. His example of complete transparency was a model for me when I cried to God for what I needed.

And my life would not have half its thrills, spills, and meaningful purpose if it weren't for Given, Angel, and Tyler. They are my heart.

I must also thank my dad, Junior Gilbert, for showing me how to love, as well as giving me examples of what to do in life as well as what not to do. I owe everything to him. He helped mold me into who I am today, warts and all.

God blessed me on this writing journey with amazing companions—especially with editors and good friends, Lynne Cosby, Bethany Jett, and Jessica Everson. Their patience with me has allowed me to flourish, and their tenacity pulled the best out of me when I thought I had nothing more to give. I first met Lynne on May 19, 2011. Instead of meeting me at Starbucks, she first picked me up at my home because I had not yet been given the medical clearance to drive. As we drank our coffee, we discussed the possibilities of working together on this project. The project and I have changed over the course of our relationship. I no longer need to wrap my head in a scarf.

I was "Bethanized" when I met Bethany at a writers conference in May 2016. Her energy and clear vision knocked my socks off. And working with her, this book has morphed three times over.

I knew from the beginning that God had brought both Lynne and Bethany into my life for more than to collaborate on this writing project. These are truly two women who have changed my life—apart from writing—and I have been blessed because of them.

Then I met Jessica. She shook out the chaff, pulled the weeds, and tended to this manuscript like it was her own. Without her, this work would have stayed in the drawer, never to see light.

I am thankful for all the encouragement and gentle instruction I've received along the way. I am thankful for the opportunity to attend the Blue Ridge Mountain Christian Writers Conference and meet some folks who will be friends for life. I'm also thankful to Eva Marie Everson and Word Weavers International for offering a writers critique group for steady guidance along the way.

I would be remiss if I failed to express my gratitude to the staff assigned to me at Holy Spirit Hospital in Camp Hill, Pennsylvania and the Pinnacle Health System Community Campus, in Harrisburg, Pennsylvania. When I arrived at Holy Spirit after my seizure, I was given excellent care. At Pinnacle Health, after my surgery, even in my delicate state, I was very cognizant that each staff member I came across was valued by their peers. That may seem trivial, but it gave me the confidence that each person's skill level far surpassed adequate. The best word to describe each person I encountered is *confident*.

My neurosurgeon, Dr. Stephen Powers, was also confident; his assistant, Dr. Jay Forman, confident as well. These two men expressed no need for arrogance; just a calming assurance in their ability, as well as the ability of the team around them, to get the job done. My gratitude reaches out to all the team players; nurses, advocates, students, therapists, cleaning staff ... everyone had a responsibility that was taken seriously and appreciated by all. I have forgotten names but will never forget their hours of dedication to my needs and care.

Helping me process my journey from the beginning through to even today was my church family at Lighthouse Church in Harrisburg, Pennsylvania. Under the leadership of Pastor Kevin Brown, God's love was magnified and displayed through their acts of support and kindness. And I knew these people were praying for me; I could feel it.

I am grateful for all the supportive posts on the website Caringbridge.com. Each person who posted had a hand in lifting my spirits and helping me go on. I am also thankful for the Facebook group Brain Tumor Talk, founded by Rick Franzo. Rick learned early in his own journey with surviving brain surgery that it was essential to find a new sense of healthy. His motto, *Warriors never let other warriors walk alone ... ever!'* can been witnessed as Rick comforts those dealing with the ugliness from having their lives disrupted by a brain tumor. He has been helping other survivors and their families since 2009. God bless Rick.

It is not lost on me that there are many people posting their journeys of brain tumor struggles, most asking the same question— *Why?* Brain Tumor Talk is a safe place for hurting people to process their pain and frustration with others dealing with the same situations. Reading the accounts of other survivors reminds me of the blessings that wait for us all.

Thanks also go to the West Shore Christian Writers Group from Mechanicsburg, Pennsylvania, and the many people I have met and worked with at the Blue Ridge Mountain Christian Writers Conference. I found encouragement, direction, and challenge to tell the story as it needed to be told. Several times, conferees and faculty from BRMCWC stopped what they were doing to pray for me and this project. To all of my friends from my writers group and BRMCWC, I couldn't have finished this book without you.

To the people who contributed their stories to this book, I'd like to thank Donna Brown (Harrisburg, Pennsylvania), Fran Sadin, (Greenville, Texas), my friend, Sharon Tedford (currently in Dallas,

Texas), Christina Custodio (Greenville, South Carolina), and the two contributors who shared their stories from behind a veil.

Please take a moment to study the book's cover, and you'll see why I fell in love with cover designer Amber Weigand-Buckley. She's brilliant, with an eye for color and detail. You've taken my words and wrapped them in beauty.

Last, but definitely not least, are Rhonda Rhea and Karen Porter of Bold Vision Books. Rhonda saw the promise in this diamond-in-the-rough manuscript and convinced Karen to take a chance. And Karen, along with her team, have been unwavering in their support. I owe each and every one of the noted people humble gratitude for traveling with me on my God's Best writing journey.

Chariots of Fire is a story of the Olympic runner Eric Liddell who refused to race on Sundays because he believed the Bible passage that says, "For those who honor me I will honor."[29] Please know that I acknowledge my gratitude and honor to God the most. This book would not exist if God had not shown grace and mercy to me. I'm thankful for my new limitations. In my weakness, Christ's strength shines. I'm thrilled to recognize my part of this grand scheme set before us all and am watching anxiously to see the direction God wants my toes to point. What I'm trying to say is, *Thank You, Father, because you sustain me. You have provided everything I have ever needed. I look forward to the days you have waiting for me.*

---

29   1 Samuel 2:30

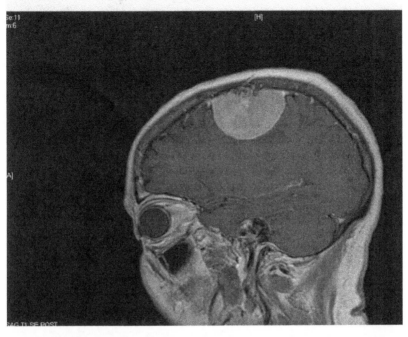

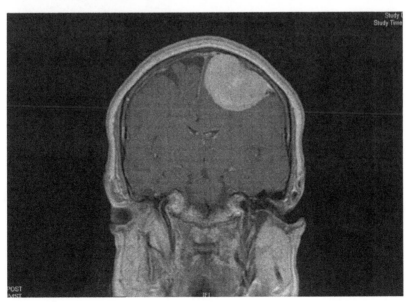

About the Author

AUTHOR ROBIN LUFTIG is founder of Renew Ministries She is also a nationally-known speaker for Stonecroft Ministries and columnist for the magazine Leading Hearts and online publications such as OneChristianVoice.com and CBN.com. Her first book *Learning to Bloom Again; Walking Through Forgiveness After Divorc*e is also available

Robin and her husband Lew have five children and live in Central PA.

Endnotes

Chapter One – Moment of Truth

1   Wolterstroff, Nicolas, *Lament for a Son*, Eerdmans Grand Rapids, 1987

2   Thomas, Gary, *Sacred Marriage: What If God Designed Marriage to Make Us Holy More Than to Make Us Happy?* Zondervan, first edition 2000

3   Chapman, Gary, *The Five Love Languages: How to Express Heartfelt Commitment to Your Mate,* Northfield Publishing, first edition 1992

Chapter Two - Confession

4   *Kopp*, Heather Harpham Kopp, *Sober Mercies: How Love Caught up with a Christian Drunk*, (Jericho Books, New York, NY, 2014).

Chapter Three - Doubt

5   Spurgeon, Charles, https://en.wikipedia.org/wiki/Charles_Spurgeon, (March 20, 2017).

6   The Spurgeon Archive, https://www.spurgeon.org/resource-library/sermons/the-desire-of-the-soul-in-spiritual-darkness#flipbook/, (March 20, 2017).

7   Lewis, C.S., http://www.cslewis.com/us/about-cs-lewis/, (March 20, 2017).

8   Lewis, C.S., *Mere Christianity* (C. S. Lewis Pte. Ltd, 1952) p. 140-141.

9   Mother Teresa, *Come Be My Light: The Private Writings of the "Saint of Calcutta". Ed. Brian Kolodiejchuk (New York: Doubleday, 2007)*:1-2.

10   Yancy, Philip, *The Question that Never Goes Away* (Grand Rapids, MI: Zondervan, 2013), 82.

11   Potok: Chaim, *My Name is Asher Lev* (New York: Alfred Knopf, 1972), 114.

Chapter Four - Focus

12   Frankl: Victor, *Man's Search for Meaning* (New York: Touchstone, 1984) 115, 75.

13   Steven Furtick, *Sun Stand Still: What Happens When You Dare to Ask God for the Impossible*, (Colorado Springs, CO: Multnomath), 2010.

14   Andy Stanley, *The Grace of God*, (Nashville, TN: Thomas Nelson) 2010.

Chapter Five - Trust

15   Daniel 3:17-18, paraphrased.

16   Habakkuk 1:5-11 paraphrased.

17   Dan Reiland, *Is Spiritual Maturity an Impossible Road?*, https://danreiland.com/spiritual-maturity-impossible-road//, Sited May 27, 2017.

18   Rilke: Rainer Maria, *Letters to a Young Poet* (Novato, CA: New World Library, 2000), 74.

19   "God testified concerning him: 'I have found David son of Jesse, a man after my own heart'" (Acts 13:22 NIV).

Chapter Six - Heartache

20   Lewis: C. S., *The Problem of Pain* (New York: Macmillan, 1962), 116.

21   Monville, Marie, *One Light Still Shines: My Life Beyond the Shadow of the Amish Schoolhouse Shooting*, Zondervan, 2013.

22   Monville, Marie, *One Light Still Shines: My Life Beyond the Shadow of the Amish Schoolhouse Shooting* (Grand Rapids, MI Zondervan, 2013), p.18-19

23   IBID, p 238.

24   Fox: Michael J., *Lucky Man* (New York, NY: Hyperion, 2005), 5-6.

25   Birdinbine, Julia, *Exclusive Kathie Lee Gifford "Thought Her Whole World Was Going to End" When She Learned of Frank Gifford's Affair*, https://www.closerweekly.com/posts/kathie-lee-gifford-frank-gifford-affair-138320/, (accessed September 1, 2019).

26   Idleman, Kyle, *Grace is Greater: God's Plan to Overcome Your Past, Redeem Your Pain, and Rewrite Your Story* (Baker Books, Grand Rapids, MI, 2017), 118.

Chapter Seven - Surrender

27   Halloran, Kevin, *D.L. Moody Quotes: Inspiring Quotations by Dwight L. Moody* https://www.kevinhalloran.net/d-l-moody-quotes/, (accessed July 20, 2019)

28   Walton, Sarah, Westherell, Kristen. *Hope When It Hurts* (Purcellville, Virginia, The Good Book Company, 2017), 110-11.

29   Lamont, Anne, *Help, Thanks, Wow: The Three Essential Prayers,* (New York, Penguin, 2012), 6-7.

Chapter Eight - Faith

30   Brownback, Lydia, *Trust—A Godly Woman's Adornment,* (Wheaton, Illinois, Crossway Books), page 30

31   Stanley, Charles, *Rebuilding Your Faith,* http://www.faithgateway.com/rebuilding-your-faith/#.WU7CT-vyvIU, accessed June 24, 2017.

32   Groeschel. Craog, *Hope in the Dark: Believing God is Good When Life is Not,* (Grand Rapids, Michigan, Zondervan), 2018, 34.

33   "Your eyes saw my unformed body; all the days ordained for me were written in your book before one of them came to be" (Psalm 139:16 NIV).

34   "Stay alert! Watch out for your great enemy, the devil. He prowls around like a roaring lion, looking for someone to devour. Stand firm against him, and be strong in your faith" (1Peter 5:8-9 NLT).

35   Furtick, Steven, *Sun Stand Still: What Happens when You Dare to Ask God for the Impossible,* (New York, Multnomah), 2010.

36   "If we confess our sins, he is faithful and just and will forgive us our sins and purify us from all unrighteousness" (1 John 1:9 NIV).

Chapter Nine - Gratitude

37   Premiere Speakers Bureau, https://premierespeakers.com/phil-hansen/bio, Sourced October 4, 2019.

38   Hansen, Phil, *Embrace the Shake*, TED Talk, 10:01, http://www.ted.com/talks/phil_hansen_embrace_the_shake, Sourced February 2013.

39   *Harvard Mental Health Letter*, Harvard Health Publications, "In Praise of Gratitude," http://www.health.harvard.edu/newsletterarticle/in-praise-of-gratitude, Sourced November 2011.

40   Tada, Joni Earechson, "Joy Hard Won," *Decision*, March 2000, 12.

Chapter Ten - Peace

41   Groeschel, Craig, *Hope in the Dark: Believing God is Good When Life is Not* (Zondervan, Grand Rapids, 2018) 137.

42   "Be thankful in all circumstances, for this is God's will for you who belong to Christ Jesus" (1 Thessalonians 5:18 NLT).

43   Ten Boom, Corrie, Elizabeth and Sherrill, John, *The Hiding Place*, (Chosen Books, a division of Baker Publishing), 1971

Chapter Eleven - Grace

44   "So if the Son sets you free, you will be free indeed" (John 8:36, NIV).

45   Silva, Chatal D, Newsweek. "Forgiveness' Is Trending After Moment Bothan: Jean's Brother Hugged Police Officer Who Killed Him and Told Her: I Don't Even Want You To Go To Jail." https://www.newsweek.com/botham-jean-brother-bryant-offers-forgiveness-hug-amber-guyger-dallas-1462868. Sourced October 4, 2019.

46   Merimee, Craig Merimee, "My End of the Road," The Merimees's Journey, February 29, 2012, http://merimeejourney.blogspot.com/2012/02/my-end-of-road.html, Sourced October 4, 2019.

Chapter Twelve – Now What?

47   Luther, Martin, "Colorful Sayings of Colorful Luther," *Christian History* No. 34, 27

48   *D'Arcy*: Paula, *Is There Life After Death?"* in *U.S. Catholic* (January 2006), 19.

49   Sittser, Jerry, *A Grace Revealed* (Zondervan, Grand Rapids, MI, 2012) 260.

50   Bengston, Michelle, *No Pain is Wasted,* Dr. Michelle Bengtson: Hope Heals, https://drmichellebengtson.com/no-pain-is-wasted/, accessed August 18, 2019.